Open the Mind,
See the Light

Translated by Wondam Sunim
Edited by Hyon Gak Sunim and Robert E. Buswell, Jr.

© 2011 by Haeun Jeongsa
Foreword © by Robert E. Buswell, Jr.
All Rights Reserved

Book designed by Gong Min Ho
Printed in the Republic of Korea by Maekyung Publishing, Inc.

ISBN No. 978-89-7442-763-4 (Limited Edition)

"Gift of Dharma - for Free Distribution"

Open the Mind, See the Light

By
Seon Master Jinje

Donghwa Monastery
Daegu, Republic of Korea

MAEIL BUSINESS NEWSPAPER

Conventions

"Seon" (also seen transcribed as Sŏn) is the Korean pronunciation of the Chinese character for "Zen," the more-familiar Japanese pronunciation of the same word. Although Seon and Zen (as well as Chinese "Chan" and Vietnamese "Thien") are simply different national pronunciations referring to the same school of Sinitic Buddhism, "Seon" is used here, since this book deals specifically with the Korean tradition of this school.

"Sunim" (more correctly transcribed as Seunim or Sŭnim) is the Korean word for a monk or a nun, and refers to any ordained cleric in the Buddhist order, from the youngest novice to the eldest Seon master. This term is used throughout this book in referring to Buddhist monks and nuns in order to convey the distinctive flavor of the Korean Seon tradition.

Korean transcriptions generally follow the latest Republic of Korea national Romanization system, which was released by the Ministry of Culture, Sports, and Tourism in 2000.

Seon Master Jinje

Geumdang Seonwon at Donghwasa

Haeun Jeongsa

Seon Master Jinje's Installation as Resident Teacher at Bongamsa

Open the Mind,
See the Light

TABLE OF CONTENTS

PREFACE

IT HAS BEEN MY PLEASURE to know Seon Master Jinje for more than 30 years. We first met at the mountain retreat of Ilta Sunim, who was renowned for his study of Vinaya and his ascetic practices. Since then, Master Jinje has come to hold a unique place in Korean Buddhist life. He was trained in the traditional monastic style of meditation which required retreat from ordinary life, but his subsequent efforts have been directed toward people living in the ever-growing urban areas of Korea. The large complex he has developed at Haeun Jeongsa is located on a mountainside at the very edge of downtown Busan. Facing the main hall, one has a view of mountains and forests. When one turns in the other direction and looks out toward the sea, there spreads out below a vast complex of high-rise buildings. One feels that his monastery is like an island floating above the busy and vibrant life of the city. The location is an expression of his attempt to preserve the values of the quietude of the mountain for reflection and contemplation while at the same time to maintain easy access for millions of people in the city below it. This combination of mountain and city is hard to create and sustain. Master Jinje has accomplished it with skill and a deep feeling of compassion for the people who live their lives in the work and stress of a modern city. One is reminded of the Ten Oxherding episodes where the final scene for the meditator is the ability to reenter the market place of human activity. In many ways the activities of his monastery reflect the need to have the enlightened ones among us. It also shows us a living example of how a contemporary Buddhist master can express the reentry to the "marketplace".

Jinje Sunim's teachings expressed in this volume are traditional and yet contemporary in application. Our mind is ever a focus for his attention because it is the mind that is the seat of experience. However, he reminds us that the search for our "mind" can never result in finding a fixed and unchanging entity. Every moment is a new experience and this is true whether we are in a mountain monastery or standing in the midst of a vast city that roars around us. The application of *hwadu*, a dialogue expressing the wisdom of a questioner and the possibility of awakening this same wisdom in a responder, is at the heart of his practice and instruction. It is the shock of the unexpected, the sharpness of the rejection of normal discourse that is needed to shatter the strong defenses and barriers so deeply embedded in our psyche. In this fashion, Master Jinje presses for the adoption of this particular approach of the Korean Seon tradition. He feels that it is essential to have the moment when sudden enlightenment floods the mind of one who is faced with the intensity of *hwadu* discourse. While meditation is often a path to this singular event, he wishes to remind us that no activity can ease one into enlightenment. A shift of such magnitude in the way our minds process experience must of necessity require a method that is radical and utterly transforming. Often we hear this described as "sudden" enlightenment but it may perhaps best be described as "whole" or "entire". This means that there is nothing omitted and no exceptions from the transformation of mentality at that moment. In this volume, he shares his thoughts and insights about this method. His goal is to bring awareness of the value of *hwadu* to people everywhere. This message is presented in poetic formulations that are as pleasing to read as they are instructive.

LEWIS LANCASTER
CHEN PROFESSOR EMERITUS OF BUDDHIST STUDIES
DEPARTMENT OF EAST ASIAN LANGUAGES AND CULTURES
UNIVERSITY OF CALIFORNIA, BERKELEY

THE KOREAN SEON (Zen) Master Jinje (b. 1934) is the teacher at the major practice monastery of Donghwasa on Palgong Mountain and the founder of his own large meditation center of Haeun Jeongsa in Busan. Jinje Sunim is widely acknowledged as being one of the two most eminent teachers of traditional Korean Seon meditation; most South Korean Buddhists, in fact, know the adage "Songdam in the north, Jinje in the south", Songdam (b. 1929) being a well-known Seon master who teaches near Incheon in the northern part of South Korea, while Jinje Sunim is the most renowned Seon master in the south of the peninsula.

Jinje Sunim's style of meditation is one of the most uncompromising in contemporary Korean Buddhism, making no concessions to the exigencies of the age or the capacities of its practitioners. His approach is no intermittent avocation, promising psychological well-being, personal satisfaction, or better relationships through an hour or two of sitting a day. Jinje Sunim instead teaches an arduous meditative way of life, which seeks to free his students from the perpetual cycle of birth and death and demands everything from his students in this pursuit. When the goal is liberation itself, how could we expect him to ask less of his students?

To achieve enlightenment, Jinje Sunim teaches a time-honored Korean style of meditation called Ganhwa Seon (also seen transcribed as Kanhwa Son): the Seon of investigating (*gan*) a "topic of inquiry", or hwadu. This Korean technique is akin to the Japanese Rinzai Seon training in koans (Zen "cases"), which is better known in the West, but it developed prior to, and completely independently from, the Japanese Zen traditions. Ganhwa Seon has been taught in Korea for over 800 years, and Jinje Sunim is considered to be the latest in a long line of Korean Seon masters who trace their lineage back to the final Indian patriarch, Bodhidharma, the putative founder of the Seon tradition, and ultimately to the person of Sakyamuni Buddha himself.

In Ganhwa meditation, Seon students are given one of the traditional "topics" (*hwadu*) from the Seon tradition and taught to focus all of their attention on examining what the Seon/Zen masters of old meant by these seemingly enigmatic sayings. Jinje Sunim himself investigated several different *hwadus* in the course of his training and often confers on his students the *hwadu*, "What was your original face before your parents gave birth to you?" As the student's inquiry into this topic deepens, the mind's inability to understand what the ancient masters meant in making such a statement engenders an intense spirit of questioning and perplexity—what the Seon tradition calls the "sense of doubt" (*euijeong*). In

Jinje Sunim's presentation of Ganhwa Seon, this questioning component is paramount and distinguishes this Korean style of meditation from other forms of Buddhist meditation commonly practiced in the West, such as *vipassana* (insight meditation). Over time, this doubt becomes so intense that the mind becomes utterly absorbed in the *hwadu*, so that one becomes oblivious to everything in one's life except this questioning. Jinje Sunim calls this state, in which the *hwadu* questioning flows continuously and effortlessly like a stream, the single-minded *samadhi* (*illyeom sammae*). The fusion of questioning and the *hwadu* into a single mass eventually creates such pressure in the mind that the doubt-mass shatters, removing the limiting point of view that is the self and opening the mind to the boundless perspective that is enlightenment. In this experience of sudden awakening, the student's mind becomes identical to the minds of the ancient patriarchs and teachers of Seon and he or she knows intuitively what the Seon masters of old meant by their enigmatic statements in the *hwadus*. Thus, the mind of the buddhas and patriarchs is passed on to yet another generation of Seon students.

More than three decades ago, I had the privilege of meeting and studying with several of the most eminent Korean Seon masters of the last generation: Gyeongbong Sunim (1892-1982) at the monastery of Tongdosa, Seongcheol Sunim (1912-1993) at Haeinsa, Wolsan Sunim (1912-1997) at Bulguksa, and especially my own teacher Gusan (Kusan) Sunim (1909-1983) at Songgwangsa.

Meeting Jinje Sunim is like seeing this last generation come back to life. Even in Korea, Jinje Sunim is the last of his kind and seeing him is like meeting in the flesh one of the classic Zen masters one otherwise finds only in books. His personality embodies the core values of wisdom and compassion that have always motivated the Korean Buddhist tradition and his teachings epitomize the Seon metaphor of the finger that points, unwavering, at the moon of enlightenment. May this book inspire a new generation of Seon students in the sense of questioning that, Jinje Sunim insists, is at the core of authentic religious practice.

ROBERT E. BUSWELL, JR.
DISTINGUISHED PROFESSOR OF BUDDHIST STUDIES
DIRECTOR, CENTER FOR BUDDHIST STUDIES
UNIVERSITY OF CALIFORNIA, LOS ANGELES (UCLA)

WHO IS THE MASTER before heaven and earth are separated?
In total stillness and serenity, not a single thing can be found.
Sakyamuni and Maitreya both emerge from this place,
Manjusri and Samantabhadra come from here, too.

Sometimes I use the six-foot golden body as a blade of grass,
And sometimes I use a blade of grass as the six-foot golden body;
Sometimes sitting high on top of a peak I watch clouds appear and
disappear,
And sometimes standing at the noisy crossroads, I go with my face
ashen and muddied.

Ultimately, what do you think of this phrase?
A Seon staff over my shoulder, not regarding other people,
I stride straight into the steep mountains and deep valleys.

JINJE BEOPWON

Seon:
The Path to
Our Spiritual
Home

The Practice of Seon Meditation

QUESTION: WHAT IS SEON (Zen) meditation? And what is the world of enlightenment that you may attain through the practice of Seon?

Answer: Seon means simply "meditation", and meditation is the direct way of returning to the true nature of mind, our original home. In our original mind, there is no difference between buddhas and sentient beings. "Buddha" simply means one who has enlightened himself to the mind's fullest brightness; "sentient beings" means the mind that remains dark and confused, trapped in the heavy cloud of discursive thoughts.

Q: Everyone is endowed with mind. But what is mind?

A: Mind functions all the time in one's everyday life. Yet we willingly endure all manner of suffering simply because we have not yet allowed the mind's light to attain its fullest brightness. We are content instead to remain enshrouded in random, distracted thinking, our consciousness a heap of thousands of mental shards, entirely controlled by the power of karmic forces. Day after day, we float along, noisily carried away by complex mental states such as pride, arrogance, jealousy, envy, greed, lust, fear, anxiety, and so on.

As we learn to practice Seon meditation and work diligently on our practice, the endless stream of discursive thoughts will eventually run out. Where that stream of thoughts evaporates, the mind's fundamental radiance shines brightly. Then our mind is brilliant and free, released from all karmic impediments. This enables us to achieve whatever we want in the world.

Any of you can reach your spiritual home in this very life, but only if you put into action the guidance you receive from a clear-eyed master who has himself had an authentic insight into his own nature. Having attained insight into your true nature, you can live in bliss in all your future rebirths.

When you arrive at the original home of your Mind, infinite worlds beyond all description will unfold.

We can describe it this way: the original home of our true nature is like the hundreds of thousands of homes in a single modern megalopolis like Seoul or New York City. The city of Seoul and the five boroughs of New York are so vast that they can accommodate millions upon millions of people. Yet how incomprehensibly vaster still is the super-megacity of the mind, which contains innumerable Seouls and New Yorks, and uncountable buddhas and bodhisatt-vas. Were you to visit such a mind-megalopolis containing these uncountable mega-cities, and knock on any door, ask-ing, "Is anybody home?" Sakyamuni Buddha and Maitreya Bodhisattva would appear on the threshold. Going from neighbor to neighbor, and knocking on any door, the same thing would happen exactly as before: Amitabha Buddha and Kshitigarbha Bodhisattva would always answer the door! Everywhere and anywhere in our minds the situation is the same: our home contains a buddha, our buddha-na-ture, and bodhisattva-consciousness.

The way of Seon meditation is so marvelous that it awak-ens you to see that the Six Rebirth Destinies of heavenly beings, human beings, titans, animals, hungry ghosts, and hell denizens are not separate from one another, and that both ordinary people and sages are not two. Once you are enlightened to your own nature, the world of suffering be-comes identical to the land of all the buddhas, where all the manifold kinds of human afflictions disappear in an instant.

When you arrive at the home of your own original mind, the whole world changes to a golden land where all the

trees and grasses are constantly gleaming. As birds sing the songs of wisdom, everyone enjoys the mellifluous realm of pure Dharma. You must simply make that world your own, and in an instant you will be forever freed from the endless cycle of birth and death.

"Dying" is merely the changing of your body in the same way as you might change from old clothes into new ones. A person enlightened to his or her true nature has no problem coming or going, whether in "life" or in "death." Even in your last moment in this physical form, there is no worry or doubt. That is because in enlightenment, originally there is no birth and death, just as in a clear autumn sky, you do not see any clouds at all.

Sometimes, when we rub our eyes strongly, or bang our head on something, we can see tiny sparkling stars vaguely floating and dancing before us. They seem so real! But actually, even while we are "seeing stars," we are not actually seeing "things": we are seeing an illusion, not things that really exist. In the same fashion, sentient beings don't see true reality, because it is constantly veiled by the illusory flower-like dream of thoughts. It is in this way that sentient beings are trapped and controlled by the continuous cycle of birth and death.

However, once we return to the home of our true nature through Seon meditation, we see the true reality of existence without any illusions of any kind. One who attains the clear view of reality as-it-is is never influenced by the coming and going of appearances of this world. Reality is incomparably clear and bright, all the time. One who has attained enlightenment thus lives in complete peace and self-confidence, anytime and anywhere, without being contaminated in the least.

It may be hard for people in the modern world to imagine such a state. But there are many stories of ancient practitioners whose insight into no-life and no-death enabled them to live freely without attachment to either.

In ancient China, there once lived a man named Lanzan. He was a Man of the Way, who had awakened to his own true nature. The king heard of his excellent spiritual virtues and insights, and sent an envoy to fetch him so he could receive his teachings in the palace. When the envoy came to Lanzan's place of practice, the Seon master was eating taros, baked on a fire made from dried cow and horse dung.

The envoy bowed three times to him and said, "By royal order of His Majesty the King, you are hereby summoned for an audience in the royal palace."

But the master paid him no heed. He merely continued eating the taros, sooty with the smoke of burned cow dung. The envoy was very surprised! He had never seen such a seemingly indifferent reaction before during his entire service to the king. After several more entreaties to the monk, each delivered with increasing energy, he finally gave up and withdrew. Mounting his horse, he returned to the palace to report to the King. Enraged at the master's insolence, the King sent the envoy back again, this time with sterner orders.

The envoy returned to Lanzan's mountain cave. Though days and weeks had passed, the master was still dressed in the same shabby rags as before, his skin covered in dirt.

His nose ran freely while he hunched over more sooty, dung-cooked taros. The envoy was amazed: "Maybe there is some mistake," he thought. "Is this truly the great man of the Way, Lanzan, the meditator, who is praised across the land?"

"Sunim," the envoy asked, "an envoy of the King is a representative of the King's presence. How do you dare not show the proper face of respect to the King through his appointed envoy! Would you mind at least wiping your runny nose?"

Without even looking up from his taros, Lanzan replied, "You silly man, why would I wipe my runny nose for you?"

The envoy was struck speechless–words such as these directed at an envoy of the King could cause a man to be imprisoned or tortured. But the envoy had no choice, as Lanzan's mind was completely unswayable. Turning his horse toward the capital, he returned to report the events to the King.

The King was enraged to see his envoy returning empty-handed. "What insolence! What arrogance!," the King bellowed, in a voice that shook the imperial chambers. "Bring this defiant monk to me now!"

In those days in China, it was an unwritten law that to

disobey the royal order three times meant beheading on the spot. Even practitioners as isolated as Lanzan knew this law. Yet when the envoy paid a third visit to him, Lanzan revealed his true attainment even before the envoy could dismount from his horse. Looking up at the imperial messenger, who was huffing and puffing from his horse-sprint across the plains and mountain valleys, Lanzan greeted him by sticking his neck out in the direction of the envoy's sheathed sword. Yet even in this gesture, he never looked up from his sooty taros. This is true freedom from life and death!

The attitude of Lanzan is a good example for us: one who is awakened to his or her own true nature certainly fears nothing from "life" and "death." But such an ancient story might seem so remote from our own situations and experiences: Where does the spiritual power come from that renders one indifferent to life and death?

Once we attain our true nature, we are–in a flash–immediately freed from the trap of "name" and "form." We are also liberated from the false thought that "life" or "death" has any substantial meaning.

Nowadays it is fashionable in certain circles to declare, "Empty your mind!" This kind of phrase is circulating in many therapy and spiritual circles; it is considered a kind of self-help axiom. But whatever conceptual value this exhortation might have, it is in fact a delusion and a lie: the mind is not some "thing" that can be emptied by simply thinking, "I wish I could empty my mind."

A deeper look shows why this is not possible. Sentient beings are entangled layer by layer in habitual mental energy built up through beginningless lifetimes. Men pursue beautiful women; women are fond of handsome men. Even average folks are deluded into wishing for money and flashy possessions. People are so accustomed to living through noisy days controlled entirely by jealousy, envy, fear, anxiety and conflict. None of these things is good or bad; they are merely the force of mental proclivities accumulated over many lifetimes, whirling around in a dizzying course through the Six Rebirth Destinies of human beings, animals, and so forth. Such a force cannot be dispelled simply by thinking, "I won't think this," or "I will empty my mind." Such inexorable forces of habit can only be removed only through hard work in meditation.

But there is a clear road ahead: single-mindedly investigate the hwadu, the great question, in whatever situation, so that you forget all the boundaries of "inner" and "outer." After a time, you will then reach the state of a "stone man," where you are ready to die at any moment for the sake of truth. Once you leave that state and come back to the world alive, you will then be able to encounter good and bad situations with impartiality, settled and clear in the strength of your practice.

Then how are you going to undertake Seon meditation? Some practicalities are in order.

First, your physical posture must be straight, and relaxed. Spread the shoulders wide. Keep your spine upright. If you sit with the back stooped or curved, or the breast-bone folding in, you cannot sit comfortably for long periods. The basis of Seon is looking into this great doubt about our existence that is generated by the hwadu. Since we should look deeply into the hwadu with a clear mind, we will not make progress if we are always contending with a sagging posture. When the proper mechanics of sitting are not observed, sitting for even half an hour will feel endlessly long. So it is extremely important, whatever our bodily condition, to establish the correct posture that serves this effort.

Secondly, we must focus our eyes on a spot about six feet in front of us and raise the stay fully relaxed and prepared to engage the great question of the hwadu. But be careful, on this point: if instead you place this question of the hwadu in your head, you may feel your vital energy, or qi, rising up into your brain. If your energy rises up into your head, you might feel headaches or dizziness. This is a common mistake that beginning meditators make.

Thirdly, be mindful of the hwadu that was presented to you by an enlightened master. More than anything else, this is the key to successful Seon practice. Those who have not yet received a hwadu may take up such hwadu questions as: "What is my true self before my parents gave birth to me?," or "The ten-thousand things return to One; to what does the One return?," or "When the Master was asked, 'Why did Bodhidharma come from the West?,' why did he answer 'The cypress tree in the courtyard'?"

So, students of meditation, take care of your great doubt about the hwadu with the earnest energy of parents who have lost their only son in a sudden accident: such a tragedy would be so terrible that they would be utterly absorbed in grief and couldn't possibly have any extraneous thoughts. Should thoughts arise during your meditation, it will only be because you are not serious and thorough enough in working on your hwadu. With a resolute attitude–"I will see who I am, for sure in this lifetime, when I have been lucky enough to encounter the Buddhadharma!"–keep eagerly questioning your hwadu. Then you will not be affected by mental dullness, discursive thoughts, or random sensory experiences.

When you are brooding over the hwadu, you may become oblivious to what others are eating or talking about when you are at the dining table with your family. If you concentrate on the hwadu you are questioning, you will become numb to the things you see and hear. Nothing will disrupt your meditation. At that point, time passes in a twinkle of an eye and your single-minded brooding keeps flowing like a stream.

Whether you are a monk or a layperson doesn't matter. You laypeople may think you are serious about sitting in meditation, but then you can't but help but think about your sons and daughters–their possibilities for education and marriage, their prospects in this changing world; the mind just seems like a vast variety of swirling, discursive thoughts. This kind of "meditation" is just killing time; it is not Seon meditation.

The same is true with monks. Though monks and nuns may have shaved their heads and left their families, if monastic Seon practitioners are concerned only with eating good food, receiving good clothes, and receiving the donations of the faithful, they will never achieve single-minded attention to their practice.

Only be concerned with the hwadu! You have to keep

wrestling with the hwadu throughout all your activities, whether you are sitting or standing, cooking rice, cleaning, gardening, or whatever. As you try over and over again to continue looking into this question during all your activities, mental dullness, discursive thinking, and thoughts of this or that will calm down on their own and, unknowingly, you will be freed from all extraneous thoughts.

Unless we make this kind of hard effort, we are just mimicking others' practice, thinking, "Let me just try this once and see what it's like." This is thousands of miles away from real hwadu practice and will leave you bored with meditation, accomplishing nothing.

To advance our meditation, we must make a strong aspiration to achieve buddhahood. Even during morning and evening services, we should always think, "May the single-mindedness of this 'great doubt' about the hwadu continue unwavering; may I attain buddhahood by seeing my true nature as quickly as possible."

Therefore, when you make such a determined aspiration each and every day, all of your proclivities of habit and your weak points of character will be cut off, in an instant. Hence ancient monks made a great vow when they undertook meditation practice, such as: "May I make an auspicious connection with an enlightened one and attain enlightenment through hearing just a single word of his instructions, so that I may become a successor in the Buddha's spiritual life and save sentient beings from suffering." All the buddhas and patriarchs of the past attained buddhahood after generating such aspirations. Not only young seekers going forward in the practice of the Great Way, but lay Buddhists, too, should also emulate these past eminences in order to realize the Great Way.

So bear this in mind: great faith, strong courage, and clear aspiration should guide your meditation practice, moment after moment. Only these will eliminate the blind spots in your practice, so that you may achieve single-mindedness. Whoever among you maintains such single-mindedness in your practice will directly see the mind's true light, regardless of age or gender. When you finally open the gate of your own mind, in a flash you will be endowed with the eighty-four thousand kinds of wisdom. You will all become buddhas and act with the same power as the buddhas. This is real Seon meditation, and the very essence of the Buddhadharma.

But how do we carry this out? Once you establish a strong grounding in sitting meditation and have learned how to work with your hwadu, your practice does not stop there. A person's meditation is truly mature when it continues not only in sitting but in any situation, at all times and in all places, whether sitting, standing, or working. Practice finally matures amid the routine of our everyday lives. When sitting, the great interior questioning on the hwadu is there with you; but when moving or engaged in the myriad activities that occupy our days, if the hwadu seems lost or far away from you, then there is something not right with your practice. Why? Because this meditation practice is not something just for quiet times, for places of stillness and repose. Meditation practice is needed most when we are pushed and pulled by the agonies and sufferings of life in this world. Meditation must be clear and strong enough that we can maintain it even as our organs fail on our deathbed. Hence you should be able to keep up with your practice not only in easy and quiet times, but also during the difficulties that arise in everyday life.

Training yourself in the proper way of sitting is the simplest way to start practicing Seon meditation. As sitting makes you feel ever more grounded in your great interior questioning on the hwadu, learn to keep the inquiry into the hwadu going throughout all your activities. Then, the single-minded attention to the hwadu will flow like a stream, twenty-four hours a day, 365 days a year. This single-minded samadhi is the genuine power of true meditation.

Life is short. Before you know it, you will be seventy or eighty years of age. Sicknesses occur with greater frequency, and you will die much sooner than you expect. At the moment of death, I have heard so many good people reflect back on their lives and lament, "I wasted my life." Yet, what is the use of regret at that moment? What purpose docs it serve? We instead must devote ourselves to Seon meditation in order to set ourselves free forever from the suffering of birth and death. Since our spiritual condition in our next rebirth will be determined according to the level of our mental clarity in this life, we should not be lazy but should try to improve in our practice, moment after moment.

I encourage you to devote yourself wholeheartedly to raising your hwadu question moment after moment, hour upon hour, building up your questioning again and again, with ever greater faith. When you continue with this kind of questioning, you will cease to be aware of what you see and hear; time will seem to have stopped. Such a state of intense absorption may continue for a week, a month, or a year, flowing constantly and unbroken like a stream; this is the single-minded samadhi. When practice is maintained like this, an auspicious catalyst may fling open the gate of truth, and you will see the true nature of reality in full clarity.

This kind of effort in Seon meditation is hard to come by, however. No matter how many times you may have been reborn in the human realm, imagine for a moment how terribly hard it is to receive correct guidance. With that in mind, an ancient sage once said, "Sentient beings are hard-pressed to meet the right Dharma because they wander endlessly, deeply involved in the negative proclivities accumulated throughout countless lifetimes." I wish that all of you may one day enjoy the great bliss of the true Dharma; and having met it, I hope you will practice it sincerely and diligently!

Today you have heard this mountain monk speak about the practice of Seon. But words without action have no value. So I ask all of you to ready yourselves to put this teaching into practice.

Turning to face the wall, check to see if your seated posture is correct, or not. With your eyes open and gazing about six feet before you on the floor, concentrate your whole mental activity on the hwadu, the great topic of inquiry.

It is important to remember that when you take up the hwadu, you must raise the hwadu in its entirety and question it lucidly. As you hold the question, you may inevitably encounter periods of mental dullness. Miscellaneous, scattered thoughts may also come and go in the mind. This is natural, especially when you first begin this practice. At such times, you must make a special effort to raise the entire hwadu question, inquiring into it thoroughly from beginning to end. Question firmly, resolutely. As you keep trying and trying, genuine questioning will eventually arise, at which point your single-minded absorption in the hwadu will continue lucidly and effortlessly. This will be true practice.

Once this single-mindedness flows lucidly, the questioning into the hwadu should be thoroughgoing as well. This means that when the questioning is thorough from beginning to end, the whole of the question should flow clearly like a stream. Then you will not be affected by what you see or hear; nothing will distract you. By stabilizing the single-minded absorption in your hwadu, enlightenment is surely at hand. But until you arrive at this place where hwadu questioning flows single-mindedly, please make a strong, determined effort!

Forward to the Great Truth:
Admonitions to Monks Entering the Formal Meditation Retreat

THE TRUTH OF THE BUDDHADHARMA is the Great Way. One sure step to this Great Way is through meditation practice. The reality of the Great Way is infinitely vast and beyond all calculation; it is the locus where all disputes, comparisons, and things of every sort are completely cut off. How hard it may seem to try to grasp that place where everything is totally cut off! It may seem as vague as grasping empty space.

So, how can we ever accomplish a job that may seem so impossible to pursue in the first place?

In seeking truth, the mental attitude you bring to your practice is essential. For those with great faith and great spiritual courage, attaining the Way is as easy as touching their nose when they wash their face in the morning; but for those without faith and karmic affinities with the Right Dharma Eye, Seon practice is as difficult as grabbing a star in the sky.

Anybody who has genuine faith can attain this Way. If you receive the teachings of an awakened master, then just go straight without stepping sideways: don't check left or right. Then you can enter the gate of truth without any major detours. Without following the directions of a keen-eyed master, you go a self-willed, even arrogant, way: though you sat for eons on eons, you would not make even the slightest progress. Since the truth of the Great Way is the place where words, thoughts, and judgments are completely cut off all at once, you have to take a step forward from all false and conditioned views. Only then will you be able to move forward to the stage of no-mind.

Actually, it is not always difficult to enter the state of no-mind, the place where thinking neither comes nor goes. Simply throw away your body and life and seek the truth with total determination. When Huike stood in the snow outside Bodhidharma's meditation cave, pleading to receive the patriarch's teachings and even cutting off his own arm to prove his determination, he showed this kind of resolution. Huike made efforts in meditation commensurate with this display of devotion, and awakened himself thereby. Huike is therefore known to us today as the Second Patriarch of Chinese Seon, succeeding the legendary wall-facing Bodhidharma. If we are similarly resolute, we will see the gate of the Great Way open wide.

For some of you, although you practice Seon meditation for a lifetime, wandering from this retreat to that, you may feel as if it has all been for naught. But that is not the fault of the teachings: this occurs merely because you do not seek the truth single-mindedly, forgetting everything else. There are many of you who will spend these precious three months of retreat making a display of sitting in Seon but inwardly lost in daydreaming and wool-gathering. What could this kind of practice possibly come to?

But when you undertake the deep interior questioning on your hwadu with the resolution, "I will get through this matter of greatest importance in my life by any means necessary," you cannot but reach a state wherein time seems to have stopped and you'll be unaware of others' talking loudly beside you. You may even forget that you are sitting in meditation. If you only keep this one thought, the single-minded attention to the hwadu will flow like a stream; then anyone can open their eye of truth.

So, in order to realize the truth of the Great Way, you must establish a firm mental attitude. You must cut off all entanglements with a slash of your mind-sword. You must be constantly indifferent to whether you are sick or not, whether the food is good enough or not, and other such trivial concerns. By devoting your life to the deepest questioning on the hwadu, no other thoughts will appear in the first place, much less stick in your mind. All discursive thoughts will be completely cut off. By holding your mind in the single-mindedness of hwadu questioning, where could there be a chance for discursive thoughts to arise? You come to concentrate on hwadu with the same intensity as you would when feeling the pain from being poked by a needle. Absorbed so completely in the hwadu, those around you might say, "He looks like such a fool. Maybe he's out of his mind." But this is not really the case.

The single-mindedness of your questioning on your hwadu must flow like a stream for days or months or years. At a certain point, when the right chance comes, at the right moment in the right situation, the mass of doubt shatters and our true nature is revealed.

In winter, the piercing cold wind blows. Once a warm breeze appears, we get the unmistakable message: "Ah, spring is coming!" In that moment, the power of winter's frigidity vanishes, and all beings turn away from it to enjoy the spring air. Hwadu practice is not different from this irrefutable law of nature. It is only because Seon practitioners do not exhaustively question their hwadu from the bottom of their hearts that they can neither generate single-minded attention to the hwadu nor see their buddha-nature; this is the case even though they may have practiced for ten years or thirty years or more. When you question your hwadu deeply, you will not feel boredom during this retreat season; you may even pass this three-month retreat completely unaware of the lapse of time.

I have sometimes observed with amusement that during this intensive three-month period of constant meditation, some monks seem to go crazy with boredom, since they are not able to leave the monastery grounds or have information from or contact with the outside world. This is not the right attitude for seekers of truth to maintain. Those who spend the retreat in this manner are just mimicking hwadu questioning. This kind of practice is of no use whatsoever, no matter how many retreat seasons you pass. You will only end up owing a heavy debt to the benefactors who are funding the retreat, and you will have great regrets when you arrive at death's door. Every practitioner should draw a hard and fast line about their reason for being here. Otherwise you will dance to the same old tired tune no matter how long you play a monk's role, be it ten years, twenty years, or until your hair turns gray.

You have to check your attitude: do you live the monk's life for the sake of supreme enlightenment, or do you do it

just to pass the time as a good-for-nothing? Check yourself and check yourself again, confirm your resolve and confirm it again; one must make up one's mind again and again to practice. Leading a monk's life with dedication and perseverance is the sure road to liberation. But if you go astray, you cannot deliver even yourself: how, then, can you expect to save sentient beings from their suffering? Renouncing the world to live a monk's life is not for your parents' glory or for the status of others who are connected to you. It is your choice. So, let go of all useless entanglements and

conflicts in your mind. If you do not cast off all the false-
hoods of this transient life, you cannot take even a single
step forward.

So, even though you may have been a monk for many
years, you must constantly return to the original resolution
that compelled you to give up worldly pleasures and leave
home to ordain. Give up behaving like a regular person; be
a fool wherever you are. A fool is full of hwadu-question-
ing, moment after moment. Think and think again just on
the hwadu, "What is this?" Once the hwadu fully occupies
your mind, there would be no problem at all with anything.
With that kind of sharp determination, you will be unaware
of either the beginning or the ending of this retreat season;
you will have no concerns about how to support yourself
until the next retreat season. You will even forget the passing needs of your own physical body. If you continue in
this manner, you will be soon be approaching the gate of
enlightenment.

The same is true for lay practitioners. Wandering like
Buddhist tourists all over the country, visiting one famous
monastery or great monk's hermitage after another–this
does not necessarily lead to spiritual progress. It is better
instead to maintain a single unshakable attitude: "There is
nothing more meritorious than seeking the radiance of my

own mind." Forget all the fake spiritual showing off and make a break with your pointless social entanglements; instead, train yourselves to carry on tirelessly every day the intensive questioning into the hwadu.

If as laypeople you have already settled down in family life, you should look after your family. This is entirely appropriate. But at the same time, you must, in your everyday life, carry forward with the deep questioning into the hwadu. By doing so, your habitual karmic proclivities and the blind spots of everyday life will disappear.

One of the most famous hwadus is: "What is my True Self before my parents gave birth to me?" This is an excellent question on which to focus your practice. Now that you have encountered the Buddha's teaching, whether you are a monk or a layperson, you must find your True Self. You must have the great grace and dignity to take off this body at the moment of your physical death. There is a "true master" (*juin-gong*) who controls the body born from your parents and who comes and goes, speaks and answers, smells and hears. Just now "it" is listening to my talk. "It" is seeing me, and "it" is feeling the temperature in this room. But while "it" is not separated from me during all the hours of every day, we pass innumerable hours and days without the slightest recognition of "it." What a foolish and pitiful existence we lead! In your deeper moments, you cannot but want to know what "it" is. So, if you undertake deep questioning on the hwadu, your meditation will unwittingly mature.

Just keep this one thought, this one question: "What is 'it'?" Whether you are cooking, cleaning, working at a business, or sleeping, at all times and at all places, you must keep this one question lucidly; then all your habitual karmic proclivities will melt away. When such a mental state occurs, whether monk or layperson, you will stand directly on the threshold of enlightenment. At that point in practice, you cannot help but become awakened.

Unlike some other religions, the Buddhadharma does not claim to come from heaven. It instead acknowledges at its core that everyone is fundamentally endowed with mind. At this mind ground, there is not the slightest difference between ignorant sentient beings and enlightened buddhas and patriarchs. Even so, confused sentient beings neither know nor make use of this mind-nature, which makes them narrow-viewed and petty, prone to all sorts of differences and disputes. What a pity this is.

Once we see the mind-ground after all of these efforts, we will have achieved exactly the same level as all that of the Buddha. In this place of complete self-realization, we are not obstructed by the various layered gongan (J. koan, "Zen conundrums") gates established by the Buddha and the awakened ones.

This is why, when seekers of the Way wanted to have their spiritual attainments examined and verified, their guiding master would present them with the gongans of the ancients in order to check their understanding. Those who are rightly awakened can point east when asked about east and point west when asked about west. But if they can't answer correctly and given an irrelevant reply, the master would know they were outsiders who still did not know the truth for themselves. Since those don't yet possess the eye of truth and thus have no real attainment can't yet say which way is north, south, east, or west, they are not up to engage in dialogue with true masters and just talk nonsense out of confusion. Holding fast to one's false view is wrong and never helpful in seeking the Great Way. So, if you are controlled by wrong views, you will waste not only your present life, but you also will be unable to make your way through the hotbed of wrong views.

Therefore, true seekers should make the firm resolution always to rely on the guidance of awakened masters in helping them to establish right views. In cases when the teacher points out your wrong view, you have to make yourself let go of it. In so doing, you will be confirmed as a great vessel who is near to the Great Way.

Please check if you have any blind spots in your mind as you go forward along the Great Way and question your hwadu to the core of your marrow.

Questions and Answers on Seon

General Questions

1. WHAT IS ENLIGHTENMENT?

Seon Master Jinje: Enlightenment means to see the mind, to see the true self that is the essence of the mind. When you attain your fundamentally awakened state, you will eventually understand all the 84,000 dharmas. To one who is truly enlightened to the nature of mind, all things are free from discrimination, which means that the infinite variety things are simply one. It is as if ten people see a thing clearly in the light of day, but at night they all see it differently. Therefore if you view the mind through its natural effulgence, everything is perfectly clear: there is no right or wrong, good or evil, merit or demerit.

2. What is an Awakened One?

Seon Master Jinje: Someone who has awakened to his or her true nature is simply a person whose lives the truth and guides all people to live in peace.

3. Why do Awakened Ones today not seem to have any supernatural powers?

Seon Master Jinje: Everyday life, as it is, is a wonder; it is a mistake to wish for anything more extraordinary than that.

4. Then what difference does it make in our lives if we were to get enlightened?

Seon Master Jinje: If you are enlightened, then everyday life flows in harmony with the truth, entirely of its own accord. You will live a simple life: when you're thirsty, you drink; when you're hungry, you eat. But people in this world are always looking for something special, even though there is nothing particularly mystical or "special" about truth itself. If you do not discriminate between self or others, and do not give rise to feelings of arrogance, pride, envy, jealousy, and conflict, then you will live a life of equanimity, enthusiasm, stability, and impartiality, treating the whole world as a single family. This kind of life is the Way and the realm of truth.

If you realize the truth, you will live in bliss every day. There will be nothing more special than drinking tea when you're thirsty, resting when you're tired, or greeting guests when they visit. These everyday acts will be enough.

Sprinkling Seon Flowers on the World

5. Why do you think modern society is trending toward ever-greater mutual distrust?

Seon Master Jinje: It is due to desire, anger, and ignorance, as well as arrogance, pride, and deception.

6. Even though the modern age has seen the rise of more and more religious groups, society seems to have become more and more corrupted. Doesn't this mean that all religions, even Buddhism, are taking us

in the wrong direction?

Seon Master Jinje: This happens only because people do not meet the right teaching. As a mountain monk, I like to recommend Seon meditation as a remedy. I wish people in the leadership classes of every society might take a meditation course first before assuming the reins of power. Eventually Seon meditation should be part of primary school education for the general public as well, so that there could be many, many enlightened beings produced in this world.

7. But will becoming enlightened actually help us change our society and our history?

Seon Master Jinje: Of course it will. If you realize your true nature, in that instant you will be completely freed from everything. Since you are freed even from the illusion of life and death, all historical and social problems become completely trivial. Those who are enlightened have a discerning eye that allows them to watch carefully over society and history. For this reason, past kings have served and supported enlightened masters as royal teachers, and thus ruled over their people with the right law. This is why it is

advisable to consult often with clear-eyed enlightened ones in order to create a just society and culture.

8. Recently heavy snowfall, earthquakes, torrential rain, and tsunamis have been occurring all around the world. These natural disasters damage not only local populations, but seem to hurt and frighten our entire interconnected global village. Why are there so many such phenomena now?

Seon Master Jinje: Human beings and the entire universe follow four natural phases of life: birth, maturation, aging, and destruction. All human beings–even those who are lucky enough to live a hundred years–at some point will experience all sorts of terrible diseases in their internal organs and pain in their four limbs. In the same way, our physical world experiences similar conditions of birth, maturation, decay, and destruction. These heavy rainfalls, volcanoes, and tsunamis are all simply natural phenomena that occur on this rotating earth. If people steadily practice Seon meditation in the course of their everyday life, and try their best to help others, all of their wrongdoings will be purified, and eventually they will escape those disasters with ease.

On Birth and Death

9. We all understand why living in the world might bring
   suffering, but what is the biggest suffering of all?

Seon Master Jinje: Birth-and-death is the biggest one.

10. For sentient beings, birth-and-death may well be
    the biggest matter. But what is death?

Seon Master Jinje: If you understand the true self, you come to know that death is but a flower in the sky; it is just like an optical illusion. You know how, when you are struck suddenly on your head, or something hits on or near your eye, phantom flowers arise like a flash of lightning? Those "flowers" are not real things, but just false, illusory images that flit here and there because of momentary eye trouble. "Birth-and-death" is just like this.

11. And yet we fear death. Isn't it something we should
    fear?

Seon Master Jinje: If you are afraid of death, you do not know the true path.

12. How can those of us who are still unenlightened conquer the fear of death?

Seon Master Jinje: All sentient beings have a fear of death. But if you are steady in your Seon meditation as you seek to find your true self in our daily life, you will gain the power of samadhi (concentration). Then when you see your true identity through the power of this insight, all fears, anxieties, and illusions will vanish in an instant. At the moment of death, you will leave your body with a clear and composed mind.

13. I was told that Buddhism teaches about rebirth. Is there really rebirth?

Seon Master Jinje: If you realize the true nature of reality, there is nothing to be reborn into the six rebirth destinies. But beings who are unenlightened will surely experience rebirth.

14. In Buddhism, sometimes we hear such adages as "birth and death are not separate," or "originally, there is no birth and no death." How do you distinguish between these two teachings?

Seon Master Jinje: The reason for birth and the reason for death are the same; that is why we say that birth and death are not two. However, in the ultimate dimension, originally there is no birth or death.

Creating the Right Conditions for Seon Practice

15. Is there any difference in the extent to which monks or nuns and lay Buddhists can practice Seon?

Seon Master Jinje: Buddhist monks and nuns have a lighter daily burden, since they are single and have no family obligations. Lay Buddhists have a heavier burden to carry in their practice, since they have families to support and to worry about. However, if you have devout faith in your practice, there should be no obstacle whatsoever. With a thoroughgoing attitude and a devout faith in seeking the right Way, through effort and perseverance you can eventually meet a clear-eyed Enlightened One to guide and inspire your meditation. It doesn't matter whether you are a monk or a layperson: you will live truly according to your occupation in the world.

16. Can we make progress in practice without keeping the precepts?

Seon Master Jinje: In order to accomplish the great way, keeping the precepts is a very important foundation. You will become enlightened only if you continue questioning your hwadu while also single-mindedly keeping the pure precepts. If you can practice like this, then all at once bright wisdom unfolds while singled-minded absorption (*samadhi*) developed. It is for this reason that the Buddha taught the three-fold path of morality, meditative absorption, and wisdom. These three are actually not separate things: they are one. If you can fulfill all these three aspects, then you are certain to become a sage, like the buddha.

17. How can we get rid of sexual desire?

Seon Master Jinje: Animals and humans alike have become accustomed to sexual habits accumulated over countless previous rebirths. Because this sort of strong habit is formed over myriad of lifetimes, it is very powerful and difficult to control. In order to get rid of this proclivity, you should make an effort to achieve single-mindedness in your meditation. If you are enlightened to your own nature, and can see through the illusory veil of love and hate, in a flash all the habitual proclivities of mind will simply vanish.

The Advantages of Seon Meditation

18. What are the advantages of Seon meditation?

Seon Master Jinje: Seon meditation can turn a sentient being into a great sage. By doing Seon, you obtain great wisdom and live in great freedom and bliss. If you practice meditation with steady regularity, then even though you may not realize your true self in this rebirth, you can at least see yourself becoming wiser day by day, and you perceive this new-found wisdom integrating seamlessly with a strong sense of responsibility for the welfare of all suffering beings. As the various conflicts of everyday life in the world naturally appear–envy, jealousy, fear, anxiety, and so forth–they will gradually melt away like a spring snow under the emerging sunlight. Then you will live in peace and die in peace and, at the moment of death, you will take on a new body in surroundings better suited to practice. Therefore, you should work hard while you are alive, and generate the aspiration for great enlightenment, so that you will be able to practice in your next life, in better karmic circumstances, in order to achieve the supreme goal of attaining the final liberation of great enlightenment.

19. As a lay Buddhist working on a hwadu, and yet also living in a keenly competitive society, it would seem difficult to survive maintaining this meditation-centered lifestyle alone. What kind of attitude should we maintain in daily life?

Seon Master Jinje: We lose so much time everyday engaged in the endless flow of pointless thought. Even so, if we were to divert even a fraction of this mental energy to questioning the hwadu, then all these delusory thoughts will melt away. If we do our best in our work and our meditation without wasting time on extraneous thoughts, we will be cultivating wisdom. If we all lived this way, the world would be a better place to live and the whole world would instantly become one family prospering in peace and mutual respect. Whoever you may be–the president, farmer, politician, male or female, old or young–you all will achieve peace of mind if you practice Seon.

20. Buddhist monks say that we lay Buddhists should live in a non-possessive way. Is it possible to live without attachment?

Seon Master Jinje: Yes, it is. If you know your true self, you know the ultimate reality so that you become one with all sentient beings, which is nothing other than realization of the absolute equality of all life. Then the world we live in becomes the pure land and all humankind is but one body in one single, indivisible family. We really don't have to fight each other any longer, but can live calmly in peace and comfort all the time.

Practice, Prayer, and Wisdom

21. Is hwadu practice done through one's own effort, or
    by relying on others?

Seon Master Jinje: The practice of meditation is abso-
lutely accomplished through one's own effort. No one can
do your meditation for you. You have to devote your own
energies to meditation practice. When intense, determined
concentration continues on the hwadu question, the hwadu
will shatter by itself, quite suddenly and without outside
intervention.

22. What do you think of prayers and mantra recitation?

Seon Master Jinje: The repetition of prayers, dharanis, and
mantras are also important spiritual work. People of lower
spiritual capacity can come to the door of Mahayana (the
"Greater Vehicle") through devotion.

23. Tell us about virtue.

Seon Master Jinje: If you do not speak ill of others and make yourself equal to anyone according to your pure nature–free from self-centeredness and arrogance–you will be respected as a virtuous one.

24. What is wisdom?

Seon Master Jinje: When you see into the nature of your mind, your mind's radiance will shine brightly. When your mind becomes bright, that is what we call "wisdom."

25. Even though sentient beings are ignorant and shrouded in delusive karmic consciousness, they have observed the universe and developed the various sciences and technologies that have led to many practical improvements in people's everyday lives. Is this different from wisdom?

Seon Master Jinje: "Wisdom" and "knowledge" are two different things. While wisdom is cultivated by looking into the original nature of your minds and recovering its inherent radiance, worldly knowledge is based on discriminating between mental concepts and configuring different things. Science results from accumulating such worldly knowledge.

Karma

26. What is "karma"?

Seon Master Jinje: To those acquainted with truth, everything they meet is the true law. But to sentient beings with no insight into the truth that lies inside their own minds, everything turns into habits and karma.

27. When did karma appear?

Seon Master Jinje: The first thought that turns against the reality of your own original nature leads inexorably to all other deluded thoughts. If you are focused on the samadhi inherent in your original nature, deluded thoughts will never arise; but as soon as even a single thought leads you astray, an infinite variety of thoughts follow. That is karma.

28. So, how can we break through karmic obstacles?

Seon Master Jinje: Though you can get rid of a portion of your karmic obstacles by repentance practices and ceremonies, the only way to completely sever the cord of karmic delusion is by breaking through to enlightenment.

29. Is it true that sensory experience only adds things to our karmic storehouse?

Seon Master Jinje: Yes, it is. If you see and hear many things, your thoughts also increase accordingly, and those thoughts will grow into habits that eventually strengthen your karmic cognition.

30. Then is it good enough just to practice in the remote mountains without indulging in sensory cognition?

Seon Master Jinje: No, it is not that simple. Without an enlightened master, you only waste your precious time and energy. So a wise seeker after the truth always goes to see an enlightened master to enquire after the right path of meditation practice.

Questions about the Seon Tradition

31. Is your stage of enlightenment the same as that of
    Sakyamuni Buddha, who awoke to his own nature
    2,500 years ago by suddenly seeing the morning
    star?

Seon Master Jinje: Enlightenment means that you have
seen your original nature. Sakyamuni Buddha got enlightened by seeing his own nature, and all the other Awakened
Ones are exactly the same. Since there is no discrimination
in the ground of true enlightenment, if anyone claims to
have been enlightened on his own without a master, he will
be called a devil, a deviant from the true teachings. Therefore for this reason, the Buddha insisted that we need to
receive certification from a master who inherited the right
Dharma flawlessly, and there can never be such a cock of
the walk who insists on self-claimed enlightenment. Therefore in order to leave no room for manipulation or lies in
the field of enlightenment, we keep up the tradition of receiving certification from an enlightened predecessor.

32. What is the reason for Bodhidharma coming from India to China?

Seon Master Jinje: He had no intention.

33. Why did he have no intention?

Seon Master Jinje: *Eok!*

Examine your Hwadu

34. On one level, it would seem that the Buddha's teaching is easy to understand since he had to appeal to people from every walk of life. However, your teachings–as well as some other patriarchs' gongan instructions–are too difficult to understand and generate no real questioning, or doubt. What should I do to penetrate those gongan teachings in order to see the world of truth with ease?

Seon Master Jinje: My words, as well as all the patriarchs' teachings, are as sharp as an arrow. Just as the Buddha con-

soled crying babies with various expedients out of his compassion, so too his forty-nine years of teachings are only
a guidebook; they are not a real teaching. The patriarchs'
teachings, to the contrary, are like a sharp arrow that pierces
straight to the heart. Teachings such as this drive practitioners deeper and deeper into their sense of questioning
or doubt. If students hear these words and can keep this
single-mindedness of questioning, then any and all karmic
forces will fade away over time. Therefore any student who
is truly engaged in this meditation should consider an ancient master's single sentence or half a phrase as a piece of
gold. You should have pure faith in those statements, do as
they instruct, and take their guidance deeply to heart.

Nevertheless, should you be conniving and skeptical like
a wild fox, even a hundred years of intensive practice will
bring no benefit. But, when you meet an Enlightened One,
with thorough faith you should receive what you are taught,
and practice consistently with an upright mental attitude.

Ven. Ananda, who was the Buddha's attendant and one
of his most learned students, heard every one of the Buddha's dharma talks over the course of his nearly 49 years
of teaching. Even so, Ananda was chagrined that he still
did not understand the real essence of the Buddha's teaching. One day, he asked the Ven. Mahakasyapa, the most

senior monk in the Buddhist order, "Mahakasyapa, we all know that the Buddha transmitted his golden robe of successorship and teaching authority to you. But did the Buddha hand down to you any special teachings that he did not transmit to the rest of us?"

In reply, Mahakasyapa called out, "Ananda!"

"Yes, brother?"

"Go knock down the flagpole in front of the monastery gate!" Ven. Ananda was at a complete loss for words. Embarrassed, Ananda climbed up on a great rock and sat down in such a precarious position that he could easily have fallen to his death at any moment. In that place he began serious meditation practice and didn't stop until he finally became enlightened.

This is the way the patriarchs treat their disciples. Sakyamuni Buddha instructed Ven. Ananda in approaches derived from his great compassion, explaining everything in words, and never stabbed him with pain. But Ven. Ananda received Ven. Mahakasyapa's Dharma transmission simply by penetrating this one phrase: "Go knock down the flagpole in front of the Monastery gate!"

As for this sort of Dharma teaching, the treasure of the buddhas and patriarchs is all the same; this is the Dharma that has been transmitted down to the present. That's why no one of small capacity strives to learn this teaching. Only a person of great spiritual capacity, who has firm faith and earnest single-mindedness, is ready to open his mind upon hearing just one word of an enlightened master. If a practitioner empties his mind and receives the full guidance of an Enlightened One, he takes the Master's treasure as his own. That is why, in order to step into the gate of the Great Way, you should throw away all your narrow understanding and knowledge. Please don't hear this story carelessly, but take it deeply to heart. Put it into practice, and you will surely gain a lot.

35. Please teach us Seon meditation so we may discover our true self.

Seon Master Jinje: All truth is found only in our true self. And there is a right way to find that truth, which is called Seon meditation. You must consider the hwadu question: "What is my true self before my parents gave birth to me?"

This body inevitably decomposes, so it cannot be our true self. So, what then is my real self before I received this body from my parents? Sakyamuni Buddha became the greatest teacher of the Way by knowing his true self; all the awakened ones were also people who simply came to know their true selves. If everyone accepts right guidance, practices daily, and attains the stage of single-mindedness in questioning meditation, their true self shall open for them, just as it did for the Buddha and the patriarchs.

This single-mindedness means that whether we cook rice, do the laundry, farm a plot of land, take a walk, work at our business, or sit through the night, we continue to keep questioning, "What was I before my parents gave birth to me?" You have simply to push the doubt "What is my true self?" a thousand times, and a thousand times after that.

When you meditate on the hwadu question "What is my true self?," don't worry or be overly anxious about the questioning itself. Sometimes, by being too "tight" about the questioning and the practice, your vital energy might shoot up right into your head, which will leave you too dull and heavy to continue with the meditation. Instead, you simply should question: "What was I before my parents gave birth to me? What is my true self? What is it?" While you are looking for your true self, the true questioning persists and continues day and night incessantly, whether you eat, work, bathe, walk, or sleep. When it flows ceaselessly like a stream, then even sitting upright for several days will feel like a single moment. In this highly ripened state, when you see or hear, you sense nothing; you are only absorbed in the hwadu, the intense interior questioning. At that point, when you least expect it, the hwadu will shatter of its own accord.

"What was I before my parents gave birth to me?" That question is where your true self will be revealed.

36. What is "Ganhwa Seon"?

Seon Master Jinje: "Ganhwa Seon" means the meditation practice (Seon) that investigates or questions (*gan*) a great topic of inquiry (*hwa*). These topics are often taken from a case (*gongan*) appearing in the classical collections of Seon literature, especially the dialogues between masters and their students. This is the meditation practice inherited from Sakyamuni Buddha and transmitted down to later generations of patriarchs up to the present generation. Ganhwa Seon has at its core this deep, earnest questioning.

37. What are the characteristics and advantages of hwadu meditation, especially as compared to other meditation techniques such as Vipassana?

Seon Master Jinje: Vipassana is also a kind of meditation. However, even though you may practice it for countless years, you would still have a lower level of enlightenment. It is impossible to achieve the supreme truth through this method. All the Buddhas and Awakened Ones have transmitted this supreme truth down to the present without interruption. To realize the highest truth is only possible through Ganhwa meditation.

The major difference between Ganhwa Seon and other forms of meditation is the special and important component called "questioning samadhi." In Ganhwa Seon, your questioning and the hwadu form one great doubt-mass, until the questioning flows uninterrupted and you become unaware whether it is day or night. Then, unexpectedly, in a single moment of seeing or hearing, the doubt-mass shatters and you experience enlightenment.

Vipassana is just observing without any questioning dimension. With Vipassana, you may also practice the deeds of bodhisattvas with pure compassion, but your power of goodness will be weak, and not strong enough to achieve great enlightenment.

38. What is the hwadu?

Seon Master Jinje: The reality publicly shown to all people by all the buddhas and enlightened masters is the hwadu ("topic") and the gongan ("case").

39. Nowadays, some say that the hwadu is just a preparatory method, a way to prepare the mind for practice. What is your view on this, Master?

Seon Master Jinje: If you practice hwadu questioning and realize it completely, then it will be a shortcut to the truth.

40. How can I receive a hwadu?

Seon Master Jinje: First do three full prostrations, empty your thoughts, and listen to the enlightened master's instructions.

41. In the past, when great masters gave a hwadu phrase to a student, they considered the receiver's capabili-

ty first. But in these days, it seems like some masters just pass out hwadus in a ready-made manner, without considering the particular spiritual capacities of the receivers. One cannot avoid the impression that giving a hwadu to a student nowadays seems a little like mass production in a factory. Hwadus given in this fashion do not motivate the receivers to raise a real question, and in many cases the hwadu might not have any effect on their minds. So please tell us whether you could offer new hwadus that would be more suitable for people today, instead of the 1,700 old Seon dialogues and stories that are traditionally used, so that we could raise the deepest questioning more easily.

Seon Master Jinje: It is only your discriminative mind that causes you to blame the hwadu for your questioning being weak. What is most important is that you receive the hwadu with complete faith. You must diligently work on it regardless of whether the teacher gives you one of the 1,700 classic gongans, or gives you a word on the spot when you ask him a question. Authentic hwadu questioning never relies on what an enlightened master elucidates to you regarding this or that.

Of course, when a student comes and asks me a question either about the fundamental meaning of the Buddhadharma or "Why did Bodhidharma come from the West?," I'll give them an answer, just as the ancient masters used to do. Then you can turn it into homework to study. But these days there are very few people who really want to work with this sort of attitude. Everyone says, "I have come to you to receive a hwadu," so there's nothing I can do except take a chance and give them a hwadu of my choosing. Therefore, when working on a hwadu, the issue is not which hwadu the teacher gave you; instead, it is how sincerely you accept it and how seriously you work on it.

42. Is it all right to meditate with our eyes closed?

Seon Master Jinje: It might be ok to meditate with your eyes closed, if you can maintain your single-minded attention on the hwadu. But in nine cases out of ten, you will instead fall into delusion and sleepiness.

43. What about the various methods for controlling the breath?

Seon Master Jinje: I don't recommend any of them. Natural breathing is the best. If you try some special technique, it might well make things more difficult for your practice. So don't worry about what kind of breathing you do; just focus on your hwadu.

44. You told us to place the hwadu directly in front of our eyes. But if the hwadu is in front and the person who holds the hwadu is behind, this doesn't this create a bifurcation between the meditative object and the meditating subject?

Seon Master Jinje: I mean only that all of your attention must be placed directly in front of your eyes. If you get familiar with placing the hwadu in front, you will be able to practice with ease whether sitting, walking, lying down, or eating: all the time you will never be without your hwadu. If you hold the hwadu in your head, it may cause your *qi*-energy to rise and make you flushed. It would then be difficult to focus on the hwadu because you would be disturbed by what you see and hear.

45. Are you saying that we should "observe" the hwadu?

Seon Master Jinje: No, observing is the wrong expression. Hwadu is not an object to watch over quietly, but something that should engender profound questioning. Genuine questioning suddenly creates absorption in the single-mindedness of no-mind samadhi; then, oneself and the outside world vanish and "I" become just a mass of questioning. This mass of questioning is then free from both subject and object.

46. If we want this mass of questioning to continue unimpeded, don't we need to make an intentional effort to maintain it?

Seon Master Jinje: No, you don't need to make effort; it continues on its own.

47. If the single-mindedness of hwadu questioning is interrupted from time to time, does this mean we won't be able to sustain the practice?

Seon Master Jinje: It is a strict rule that this single-mind-edness should continue without interruption. However, there is no set limit on how long it should continue–it could be days, months, or years; it differs from person to person. As for this mountain monk, it didn't take me so long.

Overcoming the Anxious Mind

48. What is the biggest reason that many practitioners do not achieve enlightenment, even though they might spend a lifetime at it?

Seon Master Jinje: First, those who do not succeed often have not had sufficient faith in an enlightened master. Second, they may not have received correct guidance. Anyone who wishes to reach this supreme goal should cut off all entanglements and make a firm determination to attain enlightenment.

49. Is it good for us to be examined whenever we encounter new stages in our practice?

Seon Master Jinje: Since the master's role is to listen to us and give right guidance, it is best to ask.

50. Which fault is bigger, to ask or not to ask?

Seon Master Jinje: When you want to go to Seoul, you need to go straight in the right direction, and not allow yourself to be led astray. Therefore you should take instruction from an enlightened master and go straight to Seoul without wasting any time.

51. I have a problem with sexual desire when I'm asleep. Unknowingly, it coils in the center of my mind. I think that, if I could just control it, my hwadu would be single-minded. How can I control it?

Seon Master Jinje: Especially when you are young, sexual desire can be an obstacle to practice. Humans and animals are alike due to their habitual tendencies from previous lives. All creatures are interested in sex, so practitioners need to learn to be indifferent to sex–and to money, too. Without developing such indifference, you cannot achieve enlightenment.

Just reflect in this manner: this body is composed of blood and pus that come from the four elements of earth, water, fire, and wind. It is just the same even for peerless beauties. So when you emphasize the hwadu and hold single-mindedness strictly before you, these wanton thoughts will never arise. If you are still subject to such delusions, this means you have not gained strength in your practice. For this reason, those habitual proclivities formed in your previous lives rise up unawares. If you hold on to the hwadu deep in your heart, all those disturbing thoughts will simply disappear.

52. Does age matter in getting enlightened?

Seon Master Jinje: Practice is not dependent on age, but only on how willing you are to accept guidance and hold on to the hwadu.

53. I'd like to ask about the matter of physical health. How did you manage your health before you were enlightened, how do you take care of yourself now,

and are you still holding on to the hwadu now as your physical condition changes?

Seon Master Jinje: This body inevitably falls ill, whether it is healthy or not. Everybody has a little bit of sickness all the time, so we should not allow ourselves to become attached to this body. Your body may have a stomachache, or neuralgia, or a cold, and these things always come and go. But if you hold on to your hwadu and stay with it, your stomach disorder or neuralgia can be healed. If you think, "Oh! I am so weak, or I have some disease," and are so attached to this fear that you hesitate to practice, then you will never find a way out. Therefore, if you hold on to the hwadu without thinking of weak health or minor illnesses, those things will disappear naturally if you will just stay in this single-minded practice. Your mind will be detached from its obsession with illness and, naturally, your health will improve.

Moreover, when you maintain your upright posture in sitting meditation, all physical and mental obstacles will simply disappear. Your delusions and sleepiness will vanish. Therefore, the sitting posture is very important. If you habituate yourself to a correct posture, you can practice comfortably for a whole lifetime. You will be able to sit for a long time, and you won't feel a need to switch your legs up and down when they become painful.

As for diet, never eat just rich, delicious food, but eat a well-balanced diet and, most important, do not overeat.

An enlightened master accommodates the realized state in everyday life, even though he has completed his study. This means that the treasure of enlightenment is being used in all his daily activities.

54. How many hours a night do we have to sleep?

Seon Master Jinje: For people engaged in Seon practice, 4 or 5 hours of sleep a night is enough.

55. What do you think about sitting all night long without lying down to sleep?

Seon Master Jinje: I don't recommend these difficult ascetic practices. If you could sit all night long and not fall prey to drowsiness and fatigue, it would be all right, but forcing yourself to do so will just create trouble for your practice. If you hold on to your hwadu single-mindedly, you will be able to sit all day long naturally, and sleepiness and pain will vanish. But merely imitating what you have heard about monks doing, or following what you have read in books about the enlightenment experiences of certain ancient masters–this may harm your body and is of no use to the real work of enlightenment. Your body is like a machine that needs oil, so you should sleep at night and train yourself without sleepiness and delusion.

56. What do you think of eating just once a day, before noon, as the Buddha and his disciples did?

Seon Master Jinje: The time you eat is not the issue; you should always eat moderately in order to maintain your health.

57. Do you mean that if we hold on to the hwadu correctly, then such ascetic practices as day-long sittings, keeping strict silence, and eating just one meal a day will develop naturally, without having to force things?

Seon Master Jinje: That's right. You only need to hold on to your hwadu. That is all.

Life is Like Foam on Water, Do Not Pursue Things Outwardly:

The Dharma Talks of Seon Master Jinje

The "True Self" has No Beginning or End

Ascending the high Dharma Seat, Great Seon Master Jinje raised his Seon staff over the assembly and said:

IF YOU KNOW THE TRUTH of this Seon staff, you will know that your True Self has no beginning or end. In that instant, you become a person of great freedom and enjoy the universal peace of great comfort.

> The wind blows fresh at the old ferry crossing–it is a slice of autumn.
> The moonlight and the river's color reflect each other's cold;
> Open the eyes that are sublime, pure, round, and bright:
> Know and attain the auspicious person of the True Self.

If you want to understand that your True Self has neither beginning nor end, you have to know your original face, your true self, before you were born from your parents:

"What is your True Self before your parents gave birth to you?"

'What is my True Self? What on earth is my True Self?' You should raise this question thousands of times, or tens of thousands of times, in order to maintain single-mindedness in your practice.

A long time ago in China there lived an eminent layman who had achieved enlightenment. This layman, Pang Yun (d. 808), was the foremost eye of truth among lay Buddhists since Bodhidharma introduced wall-gazing Seon meditation to China. Of course, after Bodhidharma, there were also many lay Buddhists who practiced the supreme vehicle of Seon and who also attained enlightenment. But Layman Pang was second to none in the depth of his attainment of the correct wisdom eye.

In those days, too, the Seon masters Mazu Daoyi (709-788) and Shitou Xiqian (700-790) were the matchless twin stars who enhanced the Seon Dharma all over Tang-dynasty China. For that reason, monks and lay persons endowed with faith and fearless courage rushed to meet and listen to them, in order to receive guidance in studying Seon.

One day, Layman Pang bowed to Master Shitou three times and asked, "Who is it who does not make friends with the myriad things?"

As soon as Layman Pang uttered the question, Master Shitou put his hand over his mouth. In that moment, the layman had his wisdom eye opened about eighty percent. He made a deep, formal bow in appreciation of the Master's kindness.

He subsequently went to Master Mazu's residence and asked the same question as before: "Who it who does not make friends with the myriad things?"

Mazu replied, "When you swallow in one gulp all the water of the West River, I'll tell you." With these words, Layman Pang was suddenly awakened to the mind's light, and in that instant, he attained the complete wisdom eye that was the same as the buddhas and bodhisattvas.

After becoming Mazu's disciple, Layman Pang returned home and gave away to the villagers all the treasures and property his family had inherited over generations. He built a small hut by the brook, and made a simple living by weaving and selling bamboo strainers for rinsing rice. Together with his wife and daughter, he eked out a simple existence. All the Pang family committed itself only to Seon meditation. Eventually, each of them was awakened to the eye of truth. This is the legendary story of Layman Pang and his family, which is handed down to Seon prac-

titioners today.

One day, Layman Pang decided to test his daughter Lingzhao's insight. He said, "On the tips of each and every blade of grass is the Buddha's profound truth. What does this mean?"

"Oh, dear Father," she answered, "you have practiced meditation your whole life long until your teeth turned yellow and your hair gray. How did you come to have such a vulgar view?" Saying this, Lingzhao slapped her father hard across the face.

Now, in the worldly sense, one might accuse the daughter of displaying disrespectful behavior by slapping her father. But in the light of enlightenment, that's not the case at all. In the ultimate dimension, there is no senior and junior.

Without a moment's hesitation or surprise, Layman Pang asked back, "Is that all that you understand?"

She replied, "On the tips of each and every blade of grass is the Buddha's profound truth."

If you want to perceive the inner truth of this dialogue, you must first see directly into the daughter's mind-ground. She heard her father's first question, and immediately shot back, "How did you come to have such a vulgar view?" But then her answer was identical to her father's original statement! Herein lies Lingzhao's deep enlightenment and lofty insight. Both said the same words, but the difference between them is as vast as heaven and earth.

One day, the family was gathered in a room. Suddenly, Layman Pang said, "Difficult, difficult, difficult! It is as difficult as spreading one hundred gallons of oil around a tall tree."

Layman Pang's wife immediately replied, "Easy, easy, easy! It is as easy as seeing that on the tip of each and every blade of grass is the Buddha's profound truth."

And his daughter Lingzhao responded, "Neither difficult nor easy! When hungry, eat; when tired, sleep."

These three Dharma talks reveal the entirety of the Buddha's nearly 49 years of continuous Dharma teaching.

"Difficult, difficult, difficult! It is as difficult as spreading one hundred gallons of oil around a tall tree." Which aspect of truth does this phrase express? "Easy, easy, easy! It is as easy as seeing that on the tip of each and every blade of grass is the Buddha's profound truth." Which aspect of truth does this phrase express? "Neither difficult nor easy! When hungry, eat; when tired, sleep." Which aspect of truth does this phrase express?

The Pang family was one of the most exalted families in Buddhist history. They were great laypeople and great bodhisattvas who were endowed with the same wisdom eye as that of the Buddha and the Awakened Ones. These three phrases contain all of the Buddha's teaching, so anyone who can distinguish these three phrases becomes a buddha.

As word spread throughout China that Layman Pang's family was all deeply enlightened and lived gracefully, many seekers from all over the land began to visit them. The life the Pangs led shows that there is no difference in enlightenment between monks and laity. Buddhism does not value whether you have your heads shaved or whether you wear monk's robes. The proof of attainment in Buddhist practice and life is whether or not you have a clear eye of truth–this is what is distinctive.

> One day Master Tanxia Tianran (736-824) visited Layman Pang. As he came up to the front gate, he encountered the great layman's daughter, Lingzhao, rinsing vegetables at the well.
>
> Master Tianran asked her, "Is your father home?"
>
> Lingzhao stopped rinsing, stood up without a word, and laid one hand on top of the other. Master Tianran understood what she meant and asked her again, just to test her further. "Is Layman Pang in?" Without uttering so much as a single word, Lingzhao simply let go of her hands, lifted up the basket of vegetables, placed it on her head, and walked straight home. Master Tianran left immediately.

In this silence, true speech becomes clear. We should all be able to speak such speech. If you have no ears to hear and understand such speechless speech, you are not a person of high capacity. When you realize the true depth of this Dharma dialogue, you would have to admit that the fairest of the fair in all the great land of China was not the gorgeous Queen Consort Yang (楊貴妃/Yang Guifei, 719-756), but Lingzhao. She ranks with all the buddhas and the awakened ones of the past and is said to be endowed with exactly the same ground as them.

Here is another story about Lingzhao's legendary attainment and wisdom.

> One day, Layman Pang was sitting in meditation. Lingzhao entered the room, and he said to her, "At noon today, I will enter Nirvana. Go out now and check to see if it is noon yet."
>
> Lingzhao looked outside, and returned. "Father, today we are having a solar eclipse. The sun is completely covered and out of sight."
>
> "A solar eclipse, you say? The sun cannot be seen? I'm going out to see for myself." As soon as Layman Pang went outside, Lingzhao sat on her father's meditation cushion and let go of her body: she passed away at will right at that very moment. Returning to the room, Layman Pang murmured with a smile, "You wily trickster! Oh, but well done, my precious daughter!" After seven days of

mourning and then cremating his daughter's body, he sat
down in meditation, and while sitting, he too departed
from this life.

Some time later, a neighbor visited the room, only to
find Layman Pang sitting bolt-upright on his meditation
cushion, dead. The neighbor rushed to Layman Pang's
wife, who was weeding a small plot of land.

"Lady Pang! Lady Pang! Your husband seems to have
passed into Nirvana."

Hearing this, Lady Pang simply let go of her own bodily
life, one hand still scratching at the soil with a trowel, the
other hand holding a handful of weeds.

Ah, what a wonderful and grand show! What a pleasant
and dignified life! It is owing to the potential of Seon meditation that an individual–much less a whole family–can
live such a clear, one-pointed life, where life and death are
handled at will. With the right dedication, anyone can lead
such a wonderful life–coming into this world clearly, and
leaving this world clearly. This is the most wonderful way
of all.

So, dear assembly gathered here today: Do you know the
real meaning of the Pang family's Dharma message?

There was a long silence, so the Master said:

Since you are all silent, this mountain monk has no choice but to reveal the depth of the Pang family's Dharma. Rolling up my sleeves so that I may offer a Dharma gift to all of you and in service to all the buddhas, I say: if this mountain monk were with the Pang family when they uttered these statements to each other, I would have given each one of them thirty blows with this Seon staff. And if anyone were to protest and say to me, "Yes, but Layman Pang and his family showed such a wonderful example! They have glorified the Buddhadharma for ages to come. So why do you beat them?" Then, I would answer:

> Next year a new branch emerges,
> A spring breeze blows without ever stopping.

Hitting his Seon staff on the Dharma seat, the Master descended.

The Empty Space of the Universe Emerged Long Ago

Ascending the high Dharma seat, Great Seon Master Jinje raised his Seon staff over the assembly and said:

> HEAVEN AND EARTH share the same root, the myriad things are all one.
>
> There are no dharmas outside of mind; outside the dharmas, there is no mind.
>
> All the various types of schemes are like explaining a dream in a dream.

All of you in the assembly: you must devote the rest of your lives to awakening to the truth of the Buddhadharma. If you miss your chance in this lifetime, there's no guarantee that you'll have such an opportunity in the next.

All of you in this assembly should hold the hwadu deeply in your mind and continue with your questioning; there then will certainly be a time when you will be able to enter the gate of truth. The chance to meet the Buddhadharma is rarer even than a turtle that comes across a log floating on the surface of the sea once every 3,000 years. Because you have come upon this precious opportunity, I encourage you to put every ounce of your physical and spiritual energy into your hwadu questioning, until that questioning flows unceasingly day and night, like a stream. Once heaven and earth become a mass of questioning, then all of sudden, when you see or hear something, the hwadu will shatter. You will realize your true self and, without taking a single step, you will arrive at the Buddha-land and enjoy the bliss of the Dharma together with all the buddhas. Therefore, please listen carefully to the master and put his words into practice so that you may attain awakening. Then you can repay the kindness of the donors and enjoy the pure joy of Nirvana, which is free of any trace of the six rebirth destinies.

At the end of the Goryeo dynasty, Taego Bou (1301-1381) Sunim practiced in a solitary hermitage; by practicing fearlessly and enduring many hardships, he finally attained enlightenment. He then traveled to Yuan-dynasty China with the intention of receiving the mind-seal of the Buddha, and for a year wandered all over China looking for a clear-eyed master. He finally met Seon Master Shi-wu Qinggong (1272-1352), who had inherited the Dharma

lineage of Seon Master Linji Yixuan (d. 867) and was acknowledged as the 56th patriarch in the lineage of the Buddha and patriarchs.

Bou Sunim and Seon Master Shiwu talked with each other
about the content of their breakthroughs and, in the course
of that discussion, Shiwu sanctioned Taego Bou's understanding and passed on to him the Dharma lineage of the
Buddha and patriarchs. The exchange between Taego Bou
and Shiwu Jinggong, which was free of falsity or conceal-
ment, became widely known throughout the world. Both of
these masters were respected as on a par with Bodhidharma
and their Dharma lineage has continued to be transmitted
even to this day in Korea. Through their beneficence, we
have been able to encounter the correct way of Seon meditation and commit ourselves to the Buddha's path to liberation. For this reason, the grace of the patriarch Taego is so
great that it covers heaven and earth; we recognize him as
the founding patriarch of the Seon tradition of Korea.

This is the story of Taego Bou's meeting with Seon Master Shiwu Qinggong. When he arrived in China, he went to
Shiwu's monastery and paid his respects, saying, "I have
come from Goryeo to learn your supreme Dharma." Seon
Master Shiwu then questioned Bou Sunim about a famous
story regarding Niutou Farong (594-657).

When Seon Master Niutou used to sit in samadhi, heavenly lads and heavenly maidens used to come down to serve him food and hundred of species of birds picked flower petals and piled them around him as an offering. When Niutou Sunim later visited the Fourth Patriarch Daoxin (580-651), he told the patriarch about these unusual events. The patriarch rebuked him, "What's the use of a meditation in which you're being watched over by heavenly beings, birds, and beasts? How are you ever going to know the Buddhadharma with this kind of distorted knowledge and vision?" From that point on, heavenly lads and maidens never served him again and birds never offered him flower petals.

Ordinary people would probably presume that Niutou Sunim was the greatest of masters if he had heavenly lads and maidens serving him food and various species of birds offering him flowers. But for those who understand the fundamental truth of the Buddhadharma, such occurrences are not worth much. If a person abides in that supreme place where the buddhas and patriarchs reside, even the sages cannot see him, let alone the eight classes of Dharma protectors or virtuous gods and spirits, not to mention all kinds of birds and animals.

Seon Master Shiwu brought up this story and asked Bou Sunim, "What do you think of heavenly lads and heavenly maidens serving meals to Niutou Sunim and all kinds of birds offering him flowers?"

Bou Sunim answered, "Wealth is envied by many."

After Bou Sunim gave this answer, Seon Master Shiwu asked him again, "Well then, what do you think about the fact that, after Niutou met Seon Master Daoxin, heavenly lads and maidens no longer served him food and birds did not offering him flowers?"

"If you're poor, your children become distant."

Seon Master Shiwu asked Taego Bou one more time, "Then did the empty space of the universe emerge long ago (Taego) or after that long-ago time (Taego)?"

Bou Sunim replied, "Everything emerged from that long-ago time (Taego)."

After Taego Bou gave this answer, Master Shiwu handed his Seon staff over to him, and said, "I've used this staff all my life but it is still not used up, so I entrust it to you now. Take it with you and use it to deliver sentient beings everywhere." This is how it happened that Bou Sunim inherited the right dharma of the Buddha and transmitted it to Korea.

Where did this tradition of certification start? This tradition is in fact the history of Seon, which starts from the three times that the Buddha Sakyamuni transmitted the mind.

The first time the mind was transmitted occurred during the assembly on Vulture Peak, when all the heavenly beings and the great assembly of the human world sat quietly together listening to the Dharma. At the conclusion of the discourse, Indra, the King of Heaven, presented a rare Udumbara flower to the Buddha. The Buddha received the flower and, without saying a word, held it up to show to the assembly. No one in the assembly understood what Sakyamuni meant by raising the flower–except Mahakasyapa, who simply smiled. The Buddha then said, "Mahakasyapa, this Treasury of the Correct Dharma Eye I now transmit to you."

The second time the mind was transmitted occurred during a dharma assembly in front of the Reliquary of Many Children (Bahuputraka-stupa) northwest of the city of Vaisali. Mahakasyapa arrived late for the discourse. The Buddha was sitting on the dharma seat giving his dharma talk when he noticed that Mahakasyapa had arrived. The Buddha then moved over on his seat. Mahakasyapa immediately understood what the Buddha was suggesting and joined him on the dharma seat. The Buddha then put his monk's robe around Mahakasyapa and presented him to the assembly without saying a word. Everyone in the assembly was puzzled about what had happened.

The third time the mind was transmitted occurred after the Buddha had completed forty-nine years of teaching and entered Nirvana under the twin Sala trees. Seven days later, Mahakasyapa finally returned from a propagation trip. After circumambulating the Buddha's coffin, he bowed with his hands together (añjali) and said, "Oh, guide of the three realms of existence, oh benevolent father to the four types of birth! You have always taught us that originally there is no birth, old age, sickness, or death. Aren't you deceiving us by making this show of passing away?" Right then, the Buddha kicked both his feet through the side of the thick golden coffin. Mahakasyapa once again put his hands together and the Buddha immediately pulled both feet back inside the coffin. Then, the coffin lifted up into the sky and was enveloped in the fire of the wisdom samadhi, thus cremating the Buddha in empty space.

These were the three times when the mind-to-mind transmission occurred.

What is the meaning of Sakyamuni Buddha raising the flower, sharing the dharma seat with Mahakasyapa and wrapping him with his robe, and kicking his feet through his coffin?

In order to help posterity awaken to the content of the Buddha's enlightenment, he created the 100,000 types of cases, or gongan (J. kōan), to ensure that the mind-to-mind transmission, the foundation of Seon, would continue into future generations. However, Sakyamuni Buddha also taught a special dharma gate apart from these three points of the mind transmission.

One day, the Buddha ascended his dharma seat in order to give a discourse but instead sat silently without saying a word. Seeing the Buddha sitting quietly, Mañjusri Bodhisattva came forward, prostrated three times, and said, "I observe that this is the dharma of the Dharma King." The Buddha then immediately descended from the dharma seat.

All of you who are in this assembly: what did Mañjusri observe? Do you know?

There was a long silence, so the Master said:

> The sea dries up and you can finally see the bottom,
> People die, but they don't know their minds.

Even at the time of the Buddha, these kinds of gongans were widely discussed. Although it's relatively easy to understand the three mind-to-mind transmissions, it's much more difficult to understand this gongan, "I observe that this is the dharma of the Dharma King." If you experience that blissful state which comes from breaking through this gongan, then you will understand the hundreds of thousands of samadhi and immeasurable sublime meanings, and will become the master of truth in both the heavenly and human realms.

All of you in the assembly, I, this mountain monk, would like to give you one more word regarding Taego Bou's answers, so please consider it.

Seon Master Shiwu asked this question to Seon Master Taego Bou, "Before Niutou Farong met the Fourth Patriarch, why did heavenly lads and maidens present him with food and all kinds of birds offer him flowers?" Taego Bou answered, "Wealth is envied by many." But if I were there, I would have answered like this,

"They follow each other."

If I were asked: why, after Niutou met the Fourth Patriarch, did heavenly lads and maidens no longer serve him food and birds no longer offer him flowers?, I, this mountain monk, would also answer,

"They follow each other."

Hitting his Seon staff on the Dharma seat, the Master descended.

The Whole World is My Home; Carefree, I Sing a Song of Peace

Ascending the high Dharma seat, Great Seon Master Jinje raised his Seon staff over the assembly and said:

> IN THE COURTYARD of the buddhas and patriarchs, there is never a need to point spears at each other.
> Future generations made mistake after mistake without end,
> When Truth is supreme, there is no need to transmit orders from the Son of Heaven,
> So in times of tranquillity, who needs to sing a song of peace?

Seon is the essence of the Buddhadharma. All the buddhas and patriarchs achieved enlightenment through Seon meditation. But the world of enlightenment is beyond language itself. After Sakyamuni Buddha achieved awakening, he remained sitting in the pure bliss of his meditation for three weeks, before finally saying to himself, "All dharmas are characterized by tranquil extinction and cannot be taught or transmitted with words. It would be better for me simply to enter into Nirvana right now, rather than attempt to give such a teaching." This means that Seon cannot be expounded in words and letters. The moment you open your mouth to describe it, you have already made a mistake. For this reason, an ancient patriarch said that all the sutras of the Buddha's lifelong teaching–as well as the teaching of all the ancient masters–are like "selling dog meat as mutton."

Therefore, the Treasury of the True Dharma Eye and the sublime mind of Nirvana to which Sakyamuni Buddha became enlightened were transmitted from mind to mind, separately from the scriptural teachings. In the same way, this continuous inheritance is the vitality of the Seon family and the life thread of the Buddha and the patriarchs.

From Sakyamuni Buddha to Mahakasyapa, Mahakasyapa to Ananda, Ananda to Sanavasin, and so forth, in this way the transmission has been passed on from generation to generation. And this orthodox transmitted lineage of the Buddha and patriarchs was handed down to Bodhidharma, the 28th Patriarch of Indian Buddhism and the First Patriarch of Chinese Seon.

The Seon Dharma in China flourished greatly after the appearance of the Sixth Patriarch Huineng. Since Seon Master Huineng, the tradition branched out successively into the famed Five Schools of Chan or Seon: Linji (J. Rinzai), Guiyang, Caodong (J. Sōtō), Yunmen, and Fayan. Of these five, the schools of Guiyang, Yunmen, and Fayan slowly diminished in power and influence, and eventually died out. The two schools of Linji and Caodong prospered more and more in later generations.

The present Seon Dharma lineages in Korea derive from the Linji school. The Seon Dharma was introduced for the first time in Korea during the Unified Silla kingdom. Following the Korean Patriarch Beomnang (fl. ca. 632-646) being entrusted with the Dharma Lamp by the Fourth Patriarch Daoxin (580-651), a number of monks who received Dharma transmission before the Five Chan Schools formed in China founded the Nine Mountain Seon Schools (Gusan Seonmun). But the Dharma lineage of the Nine Mountain Seon Schools thrived only for a short period during the Silla Kingdom, and slowly declined in the Goryeo dynasty.

By the end of the Goryeo dynasty, the Seon lineage was in decline. Fortunately, at that time Seon Master Taego Bou (1301-1382) aroused the essence of Seon in Korea after many years of persistent teaching and hard practice. He eventually travelled abroad to train in Yuan dynasty China. There he was confirmed and entrusted with the Seon transmission by Seon Master Shiwu Qinggong (1272-1352),

who was a Dharma heir in the Chinese Linji lineage. Taego Bou was eventually acknowledged as the fifty-seventh patriarch of the Buddha and Patriarchs' transmission lineage. Through that transmission, he became the first patriarch of the Korean Seon School, forever grounding it in the Linji lineage.

Early in the Joseon dynasty, Seon Master Taego transmitted his Dharma to Hwanam Honsu (1320-1392). Since that time, Korean Seon has carried on this authentic lineage. But the Joseon dynasty period was perhaps the darkest era in the history of Korean Buddhism: it was the official policy of successive ruling Confucian governments to promote Confucianism and suppress Buddhism. Monasteries were disestablished and monks forced to secede from the order. The authentic education lineages in Korean Buddhism were stamped out. The populace's capacity to support monks and monasteries were harshly suppressed. As a result, the Seon lineages withered substantially in the middle and latter periods of the dynasty. It is sometimes said that, for the last one hundred years of the Joseon dynasty, into the early 1900's, Korean Buddhism was in a state of hibernation.

At that time, there fortunately appeared a great spiritual hero who revived the Seon Dharma in Korea. He opened a vast new horizon for the Seon school, whose very existence as a teaching tradition hung by a thread. This monk was the Seon Master Gyeongheo (1849-1912). Many excellent practitioners were produced under his guidance. He transmitted the Seon dharma to four successors: Hyewol, Man-gong, Chimun, and Hanam. Of these four, Seon Master Hyewol's lineage was passed down to me. So I, this mountain monk, am the seventy-ninth Dharma heir of the Seon lineage of the Buddha and patriarchs.

Seon Master Gyeongheo renounced the world at the age

of nine to join the Sangha. He taught in the Buddhist seminary of Donghaksa when he was as young as 22. He was renowned for being an excellent lecturer.

One day, while on the road to visit the master who had sponsored his ordination into the order, he was caught in a ferocious downpour. He ran door to door through a local village asking to take cover, but no one would let him in. The village had been struck by a cholera epidemic and the villagers were afraid to let him in their homes lest he transmit the disease to them. He finally had to pass the night under a big tree just outside the village.

Seeing the villagers dying of cholera brought a sense of urgency home to him. He went straight back to Donghaksa, sent his students away, and locked himself in his room at the monastery to devote himself solely to his hwadu meditation.

Now, Gyeongheo Sunim's academic prowess allowed him to understand most gongans intellectually, but this was with the so-called "dry wisdom" (*ganhye*) that did not generate the sense of questioning. Only one gongan really stopped his mind in its tracks: "Before the donkey has left, the horse has already arrived." This was a famous gongan from the teachings of Chinese Seon Master Lingyun (771-853). But, as with all the great gongans, its meaning could not be unlocked through a merely intellectual approach. As a result, Gyeongheo Sunim felt, at times, as if he were facing a silver mountain or pressed against an iron wall. This gongan became his practice.

Confining himself in his bare room, Gyeongheo Sunim sat constantly. He pricked his thigh with a sharp awl when he felt sleepy. He wrapped a sharp knife to the end of a bamboo stick, and placed it directly under his chin to keep himself from nodding off. He practiced very, very hard.

His Seon practice proceeded in this manner for some three months. His spiritual condition deepened, as his six senses no longer confused him; his single-minded concentration on the hwadu continued lucidly in his mind, without interruption. One day, he heard the phrase, "Even though I be reborn as a cow, I would be a cow with no nostrils" and he instantly attained enlightenment. (A cow's nostrils would be pierced and the cow shackled to a leash, so Gyeongheo is saying he will be forever unshackled.) This event occurred in 1879, when he was thirty-one.

After experiencing enlightenment, he composed a verse:

> Hearing someone mention "a cow with no nostrils,"
> In an instant I awakened to the fact that the trichiliocosm is my home.

In June, on a country road below this Yeonam mountain,
A carefree, rustic man sings a song of peace.

So, Gyeongheo Sunim made clear the origin of the Dharma transmission he had nherited. He was a successor in the lineage of Yongam Hyeeon (b. 1783). This made him the twelfth heir of Seon Master Cheongheo Hyujeong (1520-1604), and the eighth of Hwanseong Jian (1664-1729). Enlightened Seon masters are always looking forward to meeting good disciples to whom to transmit the Dharma. Successive Dharma transmission from a master to his disciples is crucially important to preserving the right Dharma.

After enlightenment, Gyeongheo Sunim sighed greatly, because it was difficult to find a disciple of sufficient capacity and insight to inherit his robe and begging bowls, which represent the Dharma transmission.

But Hyewol Hyemyeong (1855-1928) was just such a student. After Seon Master Gyeongheo formally transmitted the lamp of Dharma to his top disciple Hyewol Sunim, he wandered from monastery to monastery, re-igniting Korean monks' ardor for enlightenment through Seon meditation. As a result, many Seon centers were opened and outstanding Seon pilgrims and itinerant practitioners appeared. Thus Seon Buddhism–which had fallen into almost

total decline under the pressure of five-hundred years of
Joseon-era repression–flowered once again.

Seon Master Gyeongheo became renowned all over the
country. One day, he realized, "I see my fame rise while I
know nothing. The world is still troubled and dangerous.
I don't know where I can possibly hide myself. If I leave
the monastery and stay in town, eating meat and drinking
liquor, I might be able to hide. But it seems like the more I
hide, the more my fame grows. That's what concerns me."
One day he just disappeared, without a word. Nobody knew
where he went. A long time passed without any sightings
of Gyeongheo Sunim. Many believe that he taught local
children in a village school, letting his hair grow long and
wearing the common clothes of a local teacher. One day in
April in 1912, he is said to have left a single stanza scrib-
bled on the wall in brush-ink.

> The mind's moon is solitary and round,
> Its light swallows the myriad forms,
> When light and objects are both forgotten,
> What then is that thing?

At the end of stanza he drew a circle, and passed into
Nirvana while lying on his right side. How sad that such a

great man passed away unnoticed!

Seon Master Gyeongheo was a totally free man who championed the Seon tradition. At the same time, he was a great master who produced a galaxy of Dharma heirs during this difficult time of government suppression, when the Dharma lineage itself was on the verge of destruction.

So, assembly: Do you fully grasp the deep meaning of Seon Master Gyeongheo? What is it? What is it? Please give me an answer!

There was a long silence, so the Master said:

> Don't think it weird if I push several more drinks on you,
> Because once we part, when shall we meet again?

Hitting his Seon staff on the Dharma seat, the Master descended.

Just Keep No-Mind

Ascending the high Dharma seat, Great Seon Master Jinje raised his Seon staff over the assembly and said:

WHEN YOU QUIET all discursive thoughts and rest in body and mind, just this is "samadhi," the seat of peace where all buddhas and patriarchs of the three time-periods of past, present, and future abide tranquilly, without even a single thought of staying. This is the "no-mind samadhi." It transcends all time and space.

> One thought-moment is an infinite eon of time;
> An infinite eon of time is one moment of thought.

Three-thousand years fly by in a moment. The past, present and future times, the myriads things and the whole universe, are present in a single thought. The samadhi in which this state is perceived as is the same for both buddhas and ordinary people alike, but people do not acknowledge it. Even a fragment of a mental activity can cloud your mind, and in this confusion, you will not be able to figure out how to break through it.

In modern Korea, there was a great man of no-mind named Hyewol Hyemyeong (1862-1937). Hyewol Sunim renounced the world at the age of twelve. He had never studied in a school. Because the master who sponsored his ordination into the order later disrobed, he eventually became connected with Seon Master Gyeongheo. It was through this auspicious karmic affinity that he arrived at the gate of Seon.

Seon Master Gyeongheo used to teach him, "Your body is temporarily composed of the four elements of earth, air, fire, and water, which can neither speak the Dharma nor hear the Dharma. Space can neither speak the Dharma nor hear the Dharma. Only that 'one thing' shining brightly right before you can speak the Dharma and hear the Dharma. What is that 'one thing' shining all by itself?"

Again and again, Gyeongheo Sunim pushed his young student for an answer: "What is it that speaks and hears the Dharma? Tell what is that 'one thing' that is formless but shining brightly on its own!"

The young monk was speechless. He was stuck in the single-minded samadhi of questioning the hwadu. Whether sitting or standing, working or even sleeping, he was never separated from this single question: "What is it?" Three years passed in this state of single-mindedness. One day, Hyewol Sunim was fashioning a straw sandal with a hammer. One moment, as he struck the hammer on the shoetree, the sharp sound completely opened his mind. Suddenly, the question of "what is this 'one thing'?" was completely resolved.

He went straightaway to Seon Master Gyeongheo, who perceived the change in his mind. Gyeongheo Sunim immediately challenged his student, asking, "What is that 'one thing' shining brightly right in front of you?"

Hyewol Sunim replied, "Neither I nor a thousand saints can know it."

Thereupon Gyeongheo Sunim shot back, "What is Hyewol?"

Hyewol Sunim walked several steps from east to west, suddenly stopped, then walked back from west to east, and stopped again. Seeing this, Gyeongheo Sunim exclaimed, "Ah, how right you are! Right! Right!"

With that, the teacher approved Hyewol Sunim's attainment. In 1902, Seon Master Gyeongheo presented his

student with a Transmission Gatha, and a written lineage record establishing him as the foremost disciple in this lineage of transmission.

Bestowed to Hyewol Hyemyeong

You realize that all dharmas,

Are unascertainable in their self-natures.

If in this wise you understand the Dharma-nature,

You see the Buddha Rocana.

Topsy-turvy, I propose from the standpoint of worldly truth,

To carve a formless seal on a blue hill,

Only thus are conventional concepts papered over.

After Seon Master Hyewol got enlightened at the age of twenty-four, he stayed on Dokseung Mountain for another twenty-seven years. When he was fifty, he moved south to examine the meditation progress of the patched-robed monks practicing there. His way of probing and examination was so characteristic that a word from "Hyewol's straw-sandal-fixing hammer" dashed the monks of the southern regions into thin air. Back in those days, this phrase was often heard in the great Seon halls of Korea.

Master Hyewol liked to enjoy a calm and easy samadhi in the midst of even the simplest daily activities, such as working long days in the monastery's rice fields. In summer months, his face was always deeply sunburned from days spent in the fields, or going to the marketplace, or weaving straw sandals. His whole life was a life of no-mind, a before-thinking existence in the midst of the flow and pace of monastic life. He was as innocent as a four-year-old boy who does not feel shame and does not attempt to figure out what others want. Like a child, he was free to do whatever he pleased.

When he lived at Seonam Monastery in Busan, the monks there decided to increase the monastery's income by clearing some land for rice cultivation, and sold in advance five *majigi* (a farmland measure, about 2,500 sq. meters) of its best-quality rice paddy to cover the land-clearing costs. But after three months had passed, only three majigis of new land had been cleared. What happened?

The reason for this is because, when the hired workers felt lazy, they would insist that the Master give them a Dharma talk. Of course, the child-like Hyewol Sunim obliged them, happily chatting with them for hours on end about the Buddha's teachings.

Some monks complained that this land-clearing project–which was designed to stabilize the monastery's finances and to provide for the monks' livelihoods–was now actually decreasing it: "Sunim, you already sold five majigis of top-quality rice paddy to pay for clearing new land, but we've only cleared three. The planting season is well-nigh upon us and we're already in deficit. At this rate, how are we ever going to improve the monastery's finances?"

The Master bellowed at them instead: "Hey, you stupid

guys! Where have the five majigis gone? The five majigis
are still there, just as they always were, regardless of who
does the farming. And anyway, haven't we seen a net increase of three majigis of new land that we never had before?"

In the light of an awakened one, there is no discrimination
between "I" and "you," and no selfish motive of "mine" or
"yours." The human race is but a single family.

Even in his old age, Hyewol Sunim often personally visited the noisy market, to procure supplies for the community
of monks. One day, while on the road to the marketplace,
followed closely by his attendant, Hyewol Sunim met a
lady selling bean sprouts by the road.

"Sunim! Please buy my bean sprouts."

So he bought a bag of bean sprouts. Seeing this, another
merchant next to her pleaded, "Sunim, I am also poor, and
have a large family to support. Would you please buy some
of my sprouts as well?"

So Hyewol Sunim bought another bag, and another, and
another–in some instances, taking pity on the sellers' poverty and desperation, he would buy four or five bags in a
day. On days like this, several bags of bean sprouts would
suddenly come into the monastery kitchen.

But his compassion did not extend only to food-vendors.

When even common street-beggars asked him for something to wear, without hesitation he would take off his robes and hand them over to them. As the beggars exchanged their rags for his clothes, he stood naked and put on their rags. He then returned to the monastery dressed in these rags, to the consternation and worry of his fellow monks, who feared for his health. It may look easy to live like this, but it actually is not. Even the slightest bit of shame or self-consciousness would prevent most of us from engaging in such selfless acts of compassion. But to a seasoned meditator like Hyewol, this sort of behavior is merely the innocent activity of the no-mind.

One day, Hyewol Sunim went to the market to prepare a traditional Buddhist memorial service for a deceased layperson in his congregation. But on the way, by chance he saw a lady crying uncontrollably, cuddling her baby in her arms. He approached her and asked why she was crying. She told him that her house had burned down in a fire, and she had nowhere to live. Without a moment's hesitation, Master Hyewol gave her all the money the monastery had given him to prepare for the memorial service.

"You can fix your house with this money."

When he returned, he found that the young monks had been waiting all day for him to return from shopping. But when they saw that he was not carrying any packages, they began to worry: "Old master, what happened to you? Nothing has been delivered yet, and now here you are, empty-handed."

Hyewol Sunim replied, "The memorial service has already been duly performed, and the deceased has gone straight to the Pure Land."

The next day, as guests crowded the monastery to attend the solemn service, they found that nothing had been prepared. There was no table heaped high with offerings to honor the ancestors, no fruits to decorate the altar. Everyone was confused.

So the congregant who paid for the memorial service went to Hyewol Sunim and asked, "Sunim, what is going on here? What has happened to the service?"

Without a moment's hesitation, Hyewol Sunim smiled politely, and explained the story of the destitute woman by the side of the road. He explained that, in honor of the deceased, he gave away the payment for the memorial service for the benefit of this suffering woman and her unfortunate child. "Because the memorial service was respectfully discharged in this way, the deceased has gone straight in the Pure Land."

After hearing the master's explanation, the host was not

only relieved, but deeply pleased and honored. He then proceeded to donate more for another service, and made plentiful offerings of foods to the community of monks. Everyone was happy!

Life in Hyewol Sunim's monastery was very harsh: The countryside was very poor, and few people had anything to donate. The monks had to work every day in the fields, engaged in back-breaking work to provide even the simplest grains for their sustenance. The Korean winters can be very harsh, so the winter retreat season was particularly difficult.

There was much work, and very little food to show for it. The monks spent many hours in exhausting work, but were then challenged to practice hours of meditation under Hyewol Sunim's keen eye. Many times, there were grumblings from some of the monks about the conditions of life in this monastery.

Now, in those days, there was a peculiar monk in the community named Gobong Sunim (1890-1962). (Gobong would later become the teacher of Seung Sahn Sunim [Sungsan Haengwon, 1927-2004], the Korean Seon master who was most active in the West.) One day, while the master was absent from the monastery, Gobong Sunim sold the monastery's only ox and used the proceeds to buy an abundance of good food and drink so the monks and he could feast to their hearts' content. When the master returned to the monastery, he discovered that the ox was gone. The next day, after the meal was over, he scolded the monks and asked, "Where is my ox? Whoever sold it should come forward!"

Gobong Sunim immediately got down on all fours and crawled around the meditation hall, baying loudly, "Moo! Moo! Moo!" Hyewol Sunim spanked Gobong Sunim on the buttocks with his fan and said, "This is not our monastery ox. Bring me my monastery ox!" The matter was never mentioned again.

There is a depth of meaning here that most people would be hard-pressed to accept. Only such an Awakened Master as Hyewol could reveal the Buddha's truth simply by laughing away an awkward situation such as this.

At that time, when Korea was under harsh Japanese occupation (1910-1945), the Japanese governor-general ruled the peninsula almost like a king. Once, Governor-General Minami Jirō (1874-1955) heard a rumor that there was an enlightened man in the southern region of Korea. He visited the monk with some subordinates. The Governor-General bowed and asked for a teaching.

"Sunim, what is the highest level of the supreme truth?"

"The supreme truth of Buddhism? Hair grows out of a

ghost's fart."

A ghost is already a nonsensical idea. But saying that a ghost farts is even crazier. And crazier still, how can a hair grow from a ghost's fart? What sheer absurdity! What it meant was beyond the governor's ken. So, greatly perplexed and surprised, the Governor-General left with his subordinates.

When the Japanese invaded Korea in 1592, Hideyoshi's marauders sought to lay claim to all the treasures and lands of the Korean people. But a strong resistance was put up by an army of monks, led by the wisdom and fearlessness of two great monks who are now considered national heroes– Seosan Daesa (Hyujeong, (1520-1604) and Samyeong Daesa (Yujeong, 1544-1610). Such awakened ones have been a menace for the Japanese ever since. After the Japanese colonized Korea by force in the twentieth-century, the Japanese governors-general sometimes preemptively sought out Korean Seon masters of high renown. The story of Governor-General Minami's humiliating interview with his colonial subject, Seon Master Hyewol, travelled far and wide. The story was even whispered in parts of Japan.

The story eventually fell upon the ears of an eager young samurai who considered himself a member of the governor-general's clique. He was enraged with the news of the insolent words this Korean monk had spoken, and immediately set sail for Korea. He rode into Hyewol's monastery and marched straight into the Seon Master's room, not bothering to take off his military boots or wait for the master to get ready. Without so much as a knock, he strode right through the door. Unsheathing his sword, he pointed directly to Hyewol Sunim's throat.

"You are Hyewol?"

"Yes, I am." The Master was unmoving.

Before the samurai could say another word, Hyewol Sunim immediately pointed over the samurai's shoulder and grimaced, as if indicating there was an intruder behind him. Instinctively reacting to the potential threat, the samurai wheeled around ferociously. In a snap, Hyewol Sunim stood up and smacked the samurai between the shoulder blades, shouting, "Now taste my sword!"

The Master's sharp wit struck through to the samurai's heart. Lowering his sword, he said humbly, "So you are as great as they say you are."

And with that, the samurai bowed ceremoniously and left.

Without a sharp sword of wisdom how can you meet such a difficult situation as this, in a flash of lightning, without hesitation? Had Master Hyewol felt the slightest fear, he would have been beheaded immediately.

Yet how much more treacherous than the samurai's gleaming sword are the swords in our minds? Pride, arrogance, envy, jealousy, greed, lust–all these states of mind become endlessly entwined around your thinking. After years and years of constant habituation, is it any wonder that you find yourself so deeply harassed?

The goal of Seon meditation is to dissolve the habitual karmic proclivities accumulated in our minds. So when we work diligently in Seon meditation, we come to live by no-mind: freed from confusing thoughts, even a hundred thousand Yamas–the King of Death–cannot haul you to hell with their hundred thousand swords slicing wildly.

Hyewol Sunim had a wonderful daily life in the monastery, which showed his pure, child-like qualities and compassionate meditation. Every day, he would climb the hill behind the monastery. He collected pine cones in large rice-bags, which he burned to heat the floor of the meditation room for all of the monks. This is the simple life he led for his final days.

There was a rest stop along the climbing path. One day, the master entered Nirvana while half-standing with a sack of pine cones slung over his back.

No other Buddha, no other awakened one, had ever entered Nirvana in this posture. If he had not attained the level of no-mind, he would not have been able to do this. It was only possible due to the power of a samadhi accumulated, day by day, keeping mind and body calm and peaceful even in the midst of daily activities. If you are full of spiritual power like Master Hyewol, when you are reborn with your old body exchanged, you will still know everything even without studying. This is only possible in the world of enlightenment. Past, present and future are empty. All three time-periods are completely interpenetrating one with another.

Seon Master Hyewol made such a miraculous final display after spending his life delivering patch-robed monks and truth seekers. He truly passed on the Dharma transmitted from Seon Master Gyeongheo.

Dear assembly gathered here today. Do you see Seon Master Hyewol, this man of no-mind?

There was a long silence, so the Master said:

> A beautiful maiden left for the heavens long ago,
> A foolish young man shut himself up in his empty room.

Hitting his Seon staff on the Dharma seat, the Master descended.

What You Call the Dao
is Not the Dao

*Ascending the high Dharma seat, Great Seon Master Jinje
raised his Seon staff over the assembly and said:*

LET US CONSIDER the true meaning of Seon, the essence of
the Buddhadharma.

> When you say Seon is Seon,
> It is like searching for life with your head cut off.
> When you say Seon is not Seon,
> It is like trying to add a point to the tip of a needle.

I ask you all: where you can find the truth of Seon?

The truth of Seon is kept deep in everyone's heart. When
you light up your mind, you will manifest the living truth
even when waving your hands or moving your feet. The
person who understands this clearly will be a king of Dharma and autonomous in all situations.

Master Unbong Seongsu (1889-1944) joined the Sangha at the age of thirteen and learned the tripitaka (three baskets), of sutra (scripture), vinaya (discipline), and sastra (exegesis). Despite his extensive textual studies, he ultimately felt that academic study alone could not take him any further into the essence of truth, so he entered the gate of Seon.

He made a long pilgrimage to the famous mountains and monasteries of Korea to receive teachings from the enlightened masters of his day. Following their instructions, he exerted himself in Seon meditation for ten years, forsaking everything else. Yet despite even this arduous effort, which earned the respect of his peers, he still couldn't achieve single-minded questioning of the hwadu.

So, when he was thirty-five years old, in 1923, he made a great aspiration before an image of the Buddha and exhausted himself with consistent prayer for 100 days in order to deepen his determination. Afterwards, he joined a winter retreat at Unmun Hermitage at Baekyang Monastery. He began the retreat with a solemn vow to risk his health even to the detriment of his physical life, if only the effort would lead to liberation and a resolution of his great questioning on the hwadu. He practiced day and night, until finally single-minded concentration on the hwadu came

Formal Dharma Lecture at Donghwasa

about clearly of itself.

A full month passed. On the full moon day during the twelfth month of the lunar calendar, by chance he went out of the front gate of the monastery at dawn to refresh himself between meditation sessions. All of sudden, his mind's light shown forth, clearly resolving the hwadu question that was stuck in his chest. He then sang the following Song of Enlightenment:

Going out the gate, suddenly the cold air cuts right to the
bone,
The thing stuck in my chest has now dropped away completely.
In the frosty wind blowing on a moon-lit night, after all the
guests have scattered,
A painted pavilion stands alone, the sound of the stream is
loud amid the empty mountains.

To have his attainment confirmed, he called on Seon Master Hyewol, one of the most esteemed masters in Korea at
that time. He asked Master Hyewol, "Where do all the buddhas of the past, present, and future, and all the patriarchs
of our Dharma lineage, stay in peace and find refuge?"

Hyewol Sunim responded with silence.

Unbong Sunim asked, "How come a dragon stays sunken
in the dead water?"

Hyewol Sunim said, "What would you do if you were in
my shoes?"

Unbong Sunim raised a whisk, but Hyewol Sunim just
shook his head, "No, no, no."

With that, Unbong Sunim responded, "Ah, Sunim, a wild
goose passed by the window long before."

At these words, Master Hyewol burst out laughing, "I

cannot deceive you! I cannot deceive you!" He was deeply satisfied with Unbong Sunim's clarity and tenacity. In this way, Master Hyewol approved Unbong Sunim's enlightenment, and formally entrusted him with the Dharma lamp of the Linji lineage. His Transmission Gatha was as follows:

Bestowed to Unbong Seongsu

> All conditioned dharmas,
> Originally are free of any conditioned characteristics.
> If you perceive all characteristics as free of characteristics,
> This is called 'seeing the nature.'

> All characteristics are originally free of characteristics,
> But this freedom from characteristics is also nonabiding.
> When you put to use this sort of principle,
> You are entitled to be called 'one who has seen the nature.'

From that point on, Unbong Sunim taught the patch-robed monks and expanded the depths of Seon practice in Korea. His Dharma teaching was the most popular at that time.

One day, thirty or forty monks of high spiritual capacity gathered at Mangwol Monastery to devote themselves to a Seon meditation retreat that would last for thirty years.

The group invited Seon master Yongseong (1846-1940) to serve as the guiding teacher; Seon master Seoku (1875-1958), the first head of the Sangha, as the eldest monk; and Seon master Unbong as the head monk. They practiced eagerly day and night. After many months had passed, Seon master Yongseong gave a Dharma talk, during which he asked the following question: "Since all the buddhas of the three time-periods do not see my true appearance, and all the awakened ones of ancient times do not see my true face, where do you see me?" The congregation was totally silent. Unbong Sunim finally stood up and answered, "Hidden in a glass jar."

Without saying anything, Master Yongseong descended from the high seat and returned to his residence.

Today I would like to participate in the two masters' dialogue and let you connect with the truth. Listen to me carefully and take my words to heart. Master Yongseong asked, "Since all the buddhas of the three time-periods do not see my true appearance, and all the awakened ones of ancient times do not see my true face, where do you see me?" Then Unbong Sunim answered, "Hidden in a glass jar." At this, Master Yongseong descended from his seat without saying anything. If I were there, I would have said, "A true lion roars a real lion's roar," before descending from my seat.

If Yongseong Sunim would have given such an answer on that occasion, the Dharma meeting would have shown even more brightly.

One day, while Unbong Sunim was attending a three-month retreat guided by the famed Seon Master Man-gong (1871-1946), the master gave a Dharma talk on the case of Seon Master Yunju Daoying (?-902).

Seon Master Yunju was esteemed throughout the land for his arduous practice and deep insight. Monks and laypeople gathered from every direction, and the master gave teachings to them every month on feast days. Now, in those days, there was a hermit who built a small hut in the vicinity of the master's monastery and stayed there for over ten years, yet he never paid respects to the master or attended his Dharma teachings.

One day, curious about this hermit's practice and attainment, the master Yunju told his attendant to visit the hermit. Finding the hermit in his cell, the attendant bowed politely, and asked, "Why have you not come to any of the Master's teachings, or even paid respects to him?"

The hermit reply was compromising, "Even were Sakyamuni Buddha himself to appear, I wouldn't listen to his teaching."

The attendant returned to Master Yunju and reported the hermit's reply. Without saying anything further, the Master prepared a set of summer clothes and ordered the attendant to offer them to the hermit.

When the attendant offered up the clothes, the hermit merely turned up his nose: "I already have the clothing my parents left me. I don't need any more. Take them back!"

Returning to the monastery, the attendant reported the entire exchange to the Master. But instead of being offended, the Master sent the attendant back on another errand, telling him to ask the hermit this question: "Sunim, what kind of clothing did you wear before your parents gave birth to you?"

At this question, the hermit was completely stuck; he couldn't say a thing. Several days later, word reached the monastery that the hermit had passed away in a sitting posture. As the monks cremated his body according to the monastic rites, five-colored rays of light shone straight up into the sky. What is more, after the fire had burned down and the monks sifted through the remaining ashes, they discovered a great many relics (*sarira*). This discovery caused quite a stir in the precincts of this mountain monastery. But Master Yunju commented on this occurrence by saying: "Leaving one's physical body while sitting in meditation or leaving relics shining forth after cremation– these acts are no better than giving a correct answer to my question." After speaking these words, the relics and five-colored lights immediately disappeared.

Seon Master Man-gong asked the assembly: "If the hermit had truly awakened his eye of truth, why couldn't he answer Master Yunju's question? And yet, if he hadn't awakened his eye of truth, how could he die while seated in meditation and produce shining five-colored rays of light from his cremated relics?" Nobody could answer Master Man-gong. After a few moments, Unbong Sunim gave the following reply: "In summer, put on light hemp clothes from Andong; in winter put on heavy cotton clothes from Jinju."

Unbong Sunim wandered season after season, from this Seon monastery to that, until finally in his old age, he wound up at Myogwaneum Monastery, located in Wolnae, near Busan. Just a month before his death, his disciple, Seon Master Hyanggok, asked him:

"Sunim, when will you leave this world and enter Nirvana?"

The old master answered without the slightest hesitation,

"I will go on the day when a rabbit's tail falls off."

Now, according to the lunar calendar, the second month of the lunar year is the Rabbit Month. So, around the end of the Rabbit Month, the Master called his students and said, "Today I will enter Nirvana, so if you have any questions, please ask now."

Then Hyanggok Sunim asked, "What is the Dao, or 'Way,' of the Buddha's teaching?"

"Whey you call the Dao is not the Dao."

"Then where is the way to Nirvana?"

"Ouch, such pain!"

"When you are gone, who shall guide us?"

In reply, the old Master sang a folk tune, tapping out a rhythm on his leg:

> "Yeo-heo, yeo-heo, yeo-heo! Ru sang-sa-di-ya,
> Farmers, don't complain of having no rain!
> Rain comes over the hill out front.
> Wearing a raincoat and bamboo hat on your head,
> Let's go weeding in the paddy field instead!
> Eul leul leul leul leul Sang-sa-di-ya!! Duridung duridung!!"

After finishing this simple song, the Master lay down. As he was dying, his disciples called out, "Sunim, Sunim!"

He looked up and chided them, "What's the use of calling me?" And with that, he entered into Nirvana. His master, Hyewol Sunim, had died in a half-standing posture, with a bag of pine cones slung over his shoulders. And Unbong Sunim died in peace on "the day when a rabbit's tail falls off." In this way, he transmitted an exquisite Dharma to his disciples. What ineffably beautiful deaths their disciples witnessed!

So, I ask all of you gathered here in this Dharma hall today: "Do any of you see Master Unbong?"

There was a long silence, so the Master said:

He who is endowed with the eye of truth becomes the master of heaven and earth.

Hitting his Seon staff on the Dharma seat, the Master descended.

A Burst of Laughter Shakes Bongam Monastery

Ascending the high Dharma seat, Great Seon Master Jinje raised his Seon staff over the assembly and said:

AS AN ANCIENT MASTER once said, "As a horse gets thin, its hair grows long. When one's wisdom is wanting, one lives in poverty." Wisdom is the source of true wealth. If you have no eye of wisdom, your vessel is not enough for fame and fortune and you might not even be able to keep the inheritance your parents left you. But if you purify your mind and become wise, wisdom will remain bright, even if the universe perishes. Your enlightened mind will create your body at will, which will make you enjoy boundless happiness.

One day when he was a young boy, my teacher, Seon Master Hyanggok Hyerim (1912-1978), followed his mother to Naewon Monastery on Cheonseong Mountain. She was travelling there to see her elder son, who had become a monk. But Hyanggok was also deeply impressed by the sincerity and calm he witnessed there. He saw the monks living in meditative peace, and this so deeply touched him that he could not help but say to his mother, "Mother, I want to be a Sunim, like my brother. Please go back to the village by yourself."

In this way my teacher joined the Sangha of monks when he was only sixteen years old. He was given a hwadu by Unbong, who was the guiding Seon Master (*josil*) of the monastery in those days. The young Hyanggok wrestled with his hwadu day and night, while still fulfilling for the next two years his arduous duty as the rice-cooker at the monastery. After a long day of cooking was over, he would clean up the kitchen area, and then sit in meditation on the floor.

One spring day, after he finished his cooking job, he was sitting in meditation when a sudden gust of wind from the valley below slammed shut the kitchen door. The loud sound caused his mind's eye to open, all at once.

In those days, Hyanggok was still a postulant who had not shaved his head to ordain. He ran straight to the residence of the Seon master. The master saw that the postulant's demeanor had completely changed. Perceiving his state of mind, the Master pointed directly at a wooden pillow lying on the floor and shouted, "Say something!"

The brash young postulant kicked the pillow away. An eighteen year-old boy kicking away the pillow of a fifty year-old master–who ever heard of such a thing? Master Unbong pressed him for an answer: "You are wrong. Speak one word!"

The boy replied, "A thousand words or ten-thousand words are but talking in your sleep. The Buddha and all the awakened ones have totally deceived me!"

Though he was only a postulant, who not received even the basic precepts of a novice, Hyanggok dared to speak the absolute truth. For anyone who has arrived at one's original home of the true mind, the root of being gives one the absolute freedom to tell the truth, without regard for petty conventions.

After this extraordinary event, the brash apprentice received sramanera (novice) ordination and the Dharma name "Hyerim" from Seon Master Unbong. He was taken care of and guided privately for ten years. At last, in 1944, just before Seon Master Unbong passed into Nirvana, he gave the young monk the Dharma name "Hyanggok" and a Transmission Gatha entrusting him with the Linji lineage in Korean Buddhism:

Bestowed to Patriarch Hyanggok Hyerim

> That figureless seal coming from the West,
> Is nothing either to transmit or receive,
> When you leave far behind both transmitting and receiving,
> The crow flies and the rabbit hops.

In 1947, Seon Master Hyanggok and several of his closest Dharma brothers embarked on a bold and unusual pact: witnessing the decline of authentic meditation practice during the thirty-five years of Japanese colonial rule, they emboldened themselves to renew and revivify Korea's Seon roots with an audacious three-year intensive Seon retreat. The leading young monks of this new generation of Korean Seon, including Seongcheol (1912-1993), Cheongdam (1902-1971), and Wolsan (1912-1997), vowed to participate in this gathering at the remote monastery of Bongamsa. They made a pact to foreswear everything they had known previously and focus solely on following an intensive regimen of daily Seon practice.

One hot summer day, while Seongcheol Sunim, Cheongdam Sunim, and Wolsan Sunim were sitting on the floor, Seongcheol Sunim asked the group a question associated with an old awakened one's teaching: "When you kill the dead completely, you will see the living. When you revive the living completely, you will see the dead. Cheongdam Sunim, do you know what this means?"

Cheongdam Sunim hesitated. Hyanggok could not answer quickly, either. This inability to answer inspired Hyanggok Sunim in his practice. It pushed him anew into single-minded questioning of his hwadu.

One day, while leaning on a stone stupa, Hyanggok Sunim achieved single-minded samadhi on the hwadu. He became absorbed in a meditation so deep that he was even unaware when he sweated in the hot sun and became soaked in the rain. At this sight, some of the other monks exclaimed, "Look at him! Hyanggok Sunim keeps his samadhi so deeply that he's even unaware of the intense rain!" The other Dharma brothers were deeply inspired and encouraged by Hyanggok Sunim's concentration.

Meanwhile, for Hyanggok Sunim, the experience was as if he had become a completely dead fool: he forgot completely seeing and hearing, dropping his sense of "self" and "object" for three weeks straight. One day, in the midst of this, while walking in the monastery compound all by himself, he happened to notice his hands swinging back and forth beside him as he walked. His mind suddenly opened into a great awakening, and he achieved the resurrection that follows the Great Death.

He then recited a Song of Enlightenment,

> Suddenly seeing both hands moving back and forth, my entire being is resurrected.
> The buddhas and patriarchs of past, present, and future are mere flowers in one's eyes,
> The thousands of sutras and the myriad commentaries—what are they?
> This is why all the buddhas and patriarchs lost their lives.

> Laughing out loud in Bongamsa is a joy forever,
> The manifold tunes of Hwiyang Mountain are carefree for myriad eons.
> The full moon will shine in the next year as well.
> A crane calls anew where an autumnal breeze blows.

Hyanggok Sunim immediately called out to Seongcheol Sunim, "'When you kill the dead completely, you will see the living. When you revive the living completely, you will see the dead.' Remember when you asked me what it means? Now it's your turn to answer my question."

But Seongcheol Sunim hesitated and could not answer. Both were of the same age, born in 1912, and had been close friends since their twenties. But because Seongcheol could not answer the question he'd had the audacity to pose to the other monks, Hyanggok bawled him out, and asked him a question.

There is an important story behind the question.

> In the Tang dynasty, there lived an eminent teacher by the name of Guishan Lingyu (771-853), who led an assembly of 1,500 Seon monks. His assembly included two prominent disciples, Yangshan Huiji (813-890) and Xiangyan Zhixian (?-898). They were like dutiful sons, and would visit their Master's chambers every morning, without fail. One morning, Master Guishan was lying quietly on his bed when his devoted disciples came into the room to ask after him. After they both bowed three times in greeting, Yangshan asked him, "Master, did you enjoy a restful sleep last night?"
>
> Master Guishan simply turned on his side and said, "I had a dream last night. Do you understand my dream?"
>
> At this, Yangshan went out of the room, filled a washbasin with warm water, and placed it before the Master so that he could wash his face.
>
> Xiangyan then asked the Master, "Master, how did you pass the night?"

"Oh, I had a dream last night. Do you understand what kind of dream I had last night?"

Without a moment hesitation, Xiangyan went out and boiled a pot of tea to serve the Master. Guishan smiled: he was greatly pleased with his students and praised them both, "My dear students' quick insight and power are no less than the Buddha's two main disciples, Sariputra and Maudgalyayana."

Hyanggok told this story to Seongcheol Sunim, and asked him the meaning of this dialogue. Seongcheol Sunim hesitated again. Hyanggok Sunim bellowed, "You parasite, you're just sponging off the monastery's resources!" Hyanggok grabbed his friend by the collar, dragged him to the front gate, pushed him out, and locked the gate. "As long as you cannot respond to this dialogue, you are barred from this monastery!," he shouted.

What a great practitioner's attitude Hyanggok Sunim displayed! To take such a decisive measure, even against one's closest friend and Dharma brother, is surely hard to do. But for Seongcheol Sunim to take it to heart must have been even harder.

This all occurred when Seongcheol was 36 years old. He was kicked out of the monastery by his friend Hyanggok, who locked the gate and barred his return to the community of monks who had embarked on this three-year pact. Outside the monastery walls, deep in the mountains, Seongcheol Sunim starved for several days. He finally felt so completely mortified and chagrined that he threw himself with fearless abandon back into his meditation practice.

Finally one evening at midnight, Scongcheol Sunim's mind opened into enlightenment. He ran back to the monastery and beat the gate with a big rock. The banging noise reverberated so loudly around the monastery that it woke up the monks who were asleep in the meditation hall. Remember, this event occurred during the depths of the Korean War, so the monks were afraid that communist guerrillas had come to raid the monastery. Only Hyanggok instantly perceived the true meaning of what was happening, and he marched directly out to the front gate.

"Speak! Speak!," he shouted through the gate. "Answer correctly, and this gate will be opened."

Seongcheol Sunim gave a strong, confident answer. His eyes filling with tears, Hyanggok Sunim immediately flung open the gate. He embraced his friend, and the two danced and jumped for joy in each others' arms. What a beautiful and great scene this must have been!

Though they were Dharma brothers and the dearest of

friends, Hyanggok Sunim did not let his private feelings and affection for Seongcheol Sunim hinder what needed to be done: he pushed Seongcheol Sunim to exert himself in a fearless practice that would awaken him to his true nature. Through their friendship, mutual trust, and fearless practice, these two masters helped to open a new stage in the history of Korean Buddhism, at a time when the true wisdom eye of Seon practice was hard to find. Remembering this now, I bow to them in gratitude for their efforts to preserve and advance the teachings of Korean Seon.

From those days forward, Seon Master Hyanggok was never confused by any Dharma talks on any gongan, or by any questions posed by any of the masters throughout the land. He was free in all his Dharma speeches to give the lion's roar!

After he got final enlightenment at Bongam Monastery, Hyanggok Sunim visited great teachers all over the country. Riding as if on a matchless steed of Dharma, he rampaged everywhere, challenging practitioners and teachers wherever he went. The rumor spread far and wide that Hyanggok Sunim had passed the final level of spiritual insight. It is now said that, during those days, the right eye of Dharma opened in Korean Seon history: this was his "one road leading upward."

Following this period, Hyanggok Sunim was invited to preside as the Seon master in various monasteries. He sat together with a new generation of monks, to inspire and encourage their practice. He founded a new site for Seon practice at Myogwaneumsa in Wolnae, on the east coast of Korea. While residing therein, he made constant efforts to enhance the spirit of Korca's proud Seon traditions.

Shortly after taking up residence at Myogwaneumsa, Seon Master Hyanggok ascended the Dharma Seat and gave a talk on the "five types of samadhi."

First, grasp time and space. Take it at rest. Never let it slip out of your grasp. But do not let people in the world talk about it. This is called 'the right order' of the patch-robed monk.

Second, you must emanate light from the crown of your head. Illuminate the whole world and know clearly each and every thing in detail. This is called 'the Diamond eye' of the patch-robed monk.

Third, turn iron into gold and gold into iron. Suddenly grasp it and suddenly release it. This is called 'the Seon staff' of the patch-robed monk.

Fourth, press all the people to bite their lips and swallow their breath. And I retreat one thousand miles backward. This is called 'the vital spirit' of the patch-robed monk.

Fifth, all the buddhas in the ten directions, Manjusri and Samantabhadra bodhisattvas and all the Enlightened Ones–they all arise together at the same time and emanate a boundless light that delivers limitless numbers of sentient beings. I take a glance at it without blinking. This is called 'the specially privileged status' of the patch-robed monk.

Seon Master Jinje said, "Assembly, when you realize one by one these samadhis set up by my teacher, Seon Master Hyanggok, you will be free from everything and will never again be fooled by others' deceptions."

On another occasion, Seon Master Hyanggok gave a Dharma speech from the high seat:

Striking your walking staff like rainfall and giving a shout like thunder have nothing to do with the essence of any sort of supreme vehicle. All the buddhas of the three time-periods of past, present, and future keep it to themselves. Even the ancient patriarchs cannot show it perfectly. Volumes of Buddhist scripture cannot expound it, and an awakened patch-robed monk has nothing to do with it. Even using the word 'Buddha' is already just paying lip-service in order to accommodate regular peoples' need for some way to approach it. When you look at things frankly, even the word 'Seon' is just a mass of shame.

So, suppose that all the buddhas of the three time-periods, the ancient patriarchs, Manjusri and Samanta-bhadra bodhisattvas, all the eminent teachers and the ten-thousand sages expound Dharma until the end of time–this still would have nothing to do with the essential matter. It does not touch this matter even in the slightest! More than that, by speaking or writing about 'it,' the gap widens by thousands and thousands miles. Hence, try to elucidate the origin outside of language and letters and make clear the heart essence of the teaching outside chances and conditions; only then will you come to know of it.

If you have the slightest idea of 'Buddha' or a view of 'Dharma,' you have already gone as wide of the mark as there is space in the western sky. What shall you do then?

It's no use crying bitter tears,
Far better to spend the rest of spring with your mouth closed.

Here we can see how Seon Master Hyanggok enhanced

the Mind Seal of the buddhas and patriarchs for generations to come! He taught fearlessly like this, year after year, and as death approached, he came to stay with me at Haeun Jeongsa.

Three days before his demise, he called me to his side and left this death verse:

> A stone man on the hilltop blows a jade flute,
> A wooden maiden by the brook also dances joyfully,
> Take one step further before the ancient Buddha Majestic Voice,
> And use it without confusion for successive eons.

Subsequently, he fearlessly entered Nirvana. Thanks to his intrepid practice spirit, Seon Master Hyanggok ennobled our Seon tradition.

Well before his passing, Hyanggok Sunim once questioned me about the following story.

> After Seon Master Man-gong (1871-1946) passed away at Sudeoksa, Seon Master Yongeum took over the duty of Seon master of the monastery for five retreat seasons. After that, the position of Seon master at Sudeoksa remained vacant for several years. Seon Master Gobong

(1890-1961) was eventually invited to take the position.

One morning, Gobong Sunim was about to ascend the high Dharma seat to give a Dharma speech. Suddenly, without warning, Seon Master Geumo Taecheon (1896-1968) grabbed Gobong by the lower edges of his long ceremonial robes.

"Give us one word before you get up on that seat!"

Now, when you are asked to give a word before ascending the high seat, you had better speak out without the slightest hesitation, like a flash of lightning. Instead, Seon Master Gobong said only, "Hey, let go of my robe!"

Geumo asked again, "You must speak one word before ascending the seat."

"Let go of my robe!"

"Speak, and then you can ascend!"

"Just let go of my robe!"

Grabbing and shaking off the lower edge of a ceremonial robe–this was going on right in front of the high Dharma seat.

Forty years ago, Master Hyanggok recalled this scene, and asked me what my response would have been. "Jinje Sunim, if you had been in Gobong Sunim's shoes, what would you have answered?"

I shouted, like a flash of lightning, "*Eok!*"

Master Hyanggok checked me a little bit further. "If you shouted like that, you would have deafened all of the citizens of the city of Busan."

"Oh, that's my fault," I said.

"No, no, it's my fault," Hyanggok Sunim replied.

Today, all of you assembled here and hearing this story, do you know what it means?

There was a long silence, so the Master said:

If you can but penetrate the treasures of Master Hyanggok and me, you will easily understand this Dharma talk. When you know this kind of treasure, you will see and know correctly Hyanggok's true family tradition.

Hitting his Seon staff on the Dharma seat, the Master descended.

The Whole World is a Single Family, the Human Race is a Single Body:

A Dialogue between Seon Master Jinje and Theologian Paul Knitter

PAUL KNITTER IS THE Paul Tillich Professor of Theology, World Religions and Culture at Union Theological Seminary in the City of New York. A leading specialist in religious pluralism and interreligious dialogue, Professor Knitter is the author of many books, including Without Buddha I Could Not Be a Christian: A Personal Journey of Passing Over and Passing Back *(Oneworld Publications, 2009). Professor Knitter is especially known for bringing different religious communities together to collaborate on promoting human and ecological well-being. Because of his unique perspective on the study of both Christianity and Buddhism, Professor Knitter visited South Korea in December, 2010, in order to help foster reconciliation and dialogue between religions in Korea. During his visit, Professor Knitter visited Jinje Sunim on New Year's Eve at his monastery of Donghwasa outside the city of Daegu. This is an edited transcript of the discussion that ensued.*

SEON MASTER JINJE: SINCE THIS ROOM is blocked by a high mountain, all the buddhas and awakened ones cannot see me. Professor Knitter, how are you going to see me?

Prof. Knitter: How do I see you? Well, I see you as a representative and embodiment of a deep spiritual tradition that is even older than my own tradition of Christianity. And it is a tradition from which I know that many Christians, myself included, have learned much–I mean the Buddhist tradition in general, but especially the teachings of Zen and Seon. And I see this as a great opportunity we have now: in today's world, it is crucial that religions work together and learn from each other.

Seon Master Jinje: Oh, Prof. Knitter, you are indeed blessed! A long thread of the Buddha's mind seal is in Korea, and a strand of that thread continues right here, in Donghwa Monastery, on Palgong Mountain. This monastery preserves the favorable conditions where the supreme Dharma can be heard and practiced. Also, Donghwa Monastery has a 1600-year-old history. It is a sacred place, where some 1,450 relics of Sakyamuni Buddha are preserved and venerated.

Many Seon monks of resolute spirit are gathered here: there are 30 monks meditating in the Geumdang Seon Meditation Hall, and another 150 Seon practitioners from all walks of life meditating in the main monastery. They sit in intensive meditation for fourteen hours every day. Inspired monks from all around Korea totally devote themselves in this way, and they spend all their energy–some without sleeping–in order to inherit the Buddha's mind seal, which I myself hold. So, I deeply appreciate your visit to such a wonderful and sacred place of living practice.

Prof. Knitter: It is my honor. Sunim, one of the things that impressed me most as soon as I walked into this room was your serene and welcoming smile, the smile of enlightenment itself. I would certainly like to live the kind of contemplative life you describe going on here. If I practice as you have suggested and if I should come to an awakening about my true self, may I come back to check it with you?

Seon Master Jinje: Of course, I will welcome you with open arms. Since you have taken such a rare step as this visit, I would like to ask you to continue to soak up Korean spiritual culture to the fullest, and please spread it to the entire world!

Prof. Knitter: Oh, we want very much to do that. But we will need some help.

Seon Master Jinje: I will help you in any way I can.

Seon Master Jinje and Professor Knitter then rose from their seats and walked out to the Main Buddha Hall, where

Theologian Paul Knitter and Seon Master Jinje

a conference was being held on issues of Buddhist-Christian dialogue. There had been a heavy snowfall falling for several days, so the monastery precincts were thickly covered in white and the mountain peaks surrounding the monastery were swathed in a gleaming white blanket. As the two religious figures passed under the ancient Bong-seo pavilion, they both noticed three snowmen that visitors

to the monastery had made. Professor Knitter questioned
Seon Master Jinje.

Prof. Knitter: Sunim, are these snowmen enlightened?

Seon Master Jinje: They were even before time imme-morial. Ha!!!

Once inside the Main Buddha Hall, they took their seats, and
the conversation continued:

Seon Master Jinje: As you well know, Professor Knitter, we in Korea are in constant confrontation between North and South. In addition, the South Korean people are trou-bled by inter-religious conflict. You, as a Christian, have come from far away, bringing your great concern about the religious situation in Korea. I truly thank you for your ef-forts. Just as you are doing, all Buddhists and Christians should work together to resolve conflicts and bring peace and happiness in the world. To guide people in the right way and to strive for world peace is the responsibility and mission of us all, but especially of religious leaders.

Prof. Knitter: Well, I can speak for the many Christians who are committed to working for peace, but we always say we must work for peace together with justice. Justice must go with peace. They need each other. What many are starting to realize–and what my wife Kathy and I realized during our work in the country of El Salvador during their civil war of the 1980s–is that we must have peace in our hearts before we can have peace in the world. That is a lesson we have learned especially well from our Buddhist brothers and sisters. So just to finish, we are realizing that we must be active in our pursuit of peace, we must work at it, but we also must stop to pray, to be silent, to take care of our own spirituality. So action and contemplation, or action and meditation, must operate together.

I would like to ask you a question about what I understand to be a pluralistic dimension of all religions. My question is: We Christians believe that God can make God's truth known in many different ways. We Christians use the word "salvation": to be saved. It is similar to the Buddhist word "enlightenment." These terms seem to me to be so much alike! Now, we believe that God can save people through many different religions. In the same way, do you believe that enlightenment is possible in many religions, not just in Buddhism?

Seon Master Jinje: All religions exist for a reason, and that reason is to save the human race. Religions should guide people up the mountain of Truth. Every religion has its own characteristics, but they vary in their depths. In this troubled world, every religious leader should focus his energy simply on guiding people to the land of peace and bliss, regardless of the perceived differences in their various teachings and practices.

The Buddha teaches us that universal truth is found in our True Self. Everyone is equally endowed with the True Self. The problem is simply that people remain ignorant of their true selves, and do not harness that reality in their everyday lives.

Hence, I wish to propagate Seon practice around the world, to awaken people to the True Self that exists in their minds right now. This path is at the heart of Asian culture. Anyone who attains their True Self comes to understand that it has neither beginning nor end. The arising and passing away of everything in the universe occurs on the ground of that True Self.

Prof. Knitter: We Christians say something similar: we teach that the truth of who we really are is within ourselves; we speak about the Holy Spirit being present within us. And perhaps in the same way as you say that you are trying to realize your Buddha-nature, many Christians would say that we are trying to realize our Christ-nature, which is eternally within us.

But I might need some help in order to attain this realization. I would need someone to teach me, to guide me. I need a teacher. Of course, I find a teacher in Jesus, and I find a teacher in the Buddha. But sometimes we also may need help from "outside" to realize what we are "inside."

Seon Master Jinje: The Buddha became enlightened to his True Self. So, the practice of Ganhwa Seon, or questioning meditation, which enables people today to realize their true selves, is really nothing other than the essence of the Buddha's enlightenment. According to legend, right after Siddhartha Gautama realized his True Self, he exclaimed, "In the heavens above and the earth below, 'I' alone am venerated." This is how he demonstrated to the world that the True Self is in itself already complete and endowed with wisdom and equality. For this reason, I encourage you to take up the deep interior questioning of Ganhwa Seon so that you, too, may attain the same wisdom and equality as that of the Buddha himself.

Prof. Knitter: Well, one of the most important things that we Christians can learn from Buddhism is how to work within oneself in meditation.

So, Sunim, we have spoken about what Christians need to

learn from Buddhist practitioners like yourself. Now, with all due respect, in the spirit of this dialogue, I would like to ask if perhaps there is something that Buddhists might learn from Christians?

We Christians are beginning to realize that we need to learn from Buddhists how to be at peace, how to discover our true self through practice. But Christians also believe that it is important–it is an essential part of being "saved" or "enlightened," in fact–to act in the world and in society, to get involved in the world. We believe that it is urgent to change this world in which there is so much suffering– suffering because of social injustice, suffering because of unfair economic policies, suffering because of certain po- litical policies. This need to engage in social and political action is a part of the work of enlightenment, is it not? I am wondering whether you would agree with such a claim?

Seon Master Jinje: All Buddhists certainly admire the Protestant and Catholic practice of serving and loving your fellow man. But Buddhists take self-perfection as the pri- mary matter. When you realize self-perfection, you will au- tomatically act as a Buddha or an enlightened being. You can lead people to a land of peace and comfort. When you are not doing the inner work of becoming awakened fully to your True Self, however, you are not really able to guide people.

For this reason, as a Seon monk, I naturally strive to guide people to find their True Self by means of deep interior questioning, that is, the meditation practice that we Koreans call Ganhwa Seon. When you go up the hill of truth, you will be endowed with the eighty-four thousand dharma teachings. The sole mission of an enlightened master is to deliver everyone to the other shore of wisdom and Nirvana. Only then will you attain the point that the Buddha was referring to when he said, "In the heavens above and the earth below, 'I' alone am venerated." This insight was not something gained from a book or a tradition: the Buddha attained this view through arduous self-perfection, from his own meditation practice that looked deeply into the inner world of his mind. One taste of Korean Seon practice is enough to enable you to understand what he meant by saying, "'I' alone am venerated."

Prof. Knitter: I believe you. I know that what you say is true. But help me because I have a problem in one regard: you said that one must first realize one's true self before one goes out to act in the world for the benefit of others. You emphasize that I have to achieve Nirvana in order to do this work of helping, saving, liberating. And yet, while I am sitting, doing my meditation, children are starving and people

Seon Master Jinje

are being tortured. There is incredible racial injustice in so many parts of the world. And so, as I sit, trying to discover my true self, I cannot help but hear the cries of these suffering people. Do I really have to master this practice first before I can act? How long do I have to wait for there to be some fruit?

Seon Master Jinje: The Buddhist teachings include the two aspects of Samantabhadra Bodhisattva's "activity" and Manjusri Bodhisattva's "wisdom." There is the fully altruistic way of practice, as inspired by Samantabhadra, where one first enacts one's aspiration to deliver without omission all beings into liberation, before going on to attain one's own enlightenment. This is a very important strain of Buddhist belief. On the other hand, there is the equally valid path of holding off on such altruistic activities, and exerting oneself instead to become completely endowed with the correct eye of truth, as inspired by Manjusri's wisdom. Such an attainment would not just be "private," or "personal": it would qualify one to engage in spiritual leadership, to guide people to liberation. So, in Buddhism, these two paths exist side by side and do not exclude each other.

Prof. Knitter: So it would be correct, then, to state that we have to practice, but, at the same time, we have to act in the world; both tracks are necessary. Sunim, is it correct, then, to characterize your view as saying that, although we have both to engage others and to practice, practice is more important?

Seon Master Jinje: In the Buddhist tradition, endowing oneself with the correct eye of truth comes first. One must strive to have clear eyes first, for only then can you guide people to any kind of real liberation. If you are blind, how can you guide people to a land of peace? In that sense, we teach practitioners to "see their true natures." Since the True Self is the whole point of this teaching, seeing directly into your True Self enables you to see directly into the state of this suffering world.

In Korea, most large monasteries have established Seon meditation halls, where intrepid practitioners work hard, through intensive meditation, to awaken their correct dharma eye. Only in this way can we lead people to a land of bliss.

Now, spiritual seekers in every Seon meditation hall throughout Korea focus their efforts on "see your true nature and become a buddha." In order for them to engage in this long and lonely practice, many supporting personnel–such as abbots and monastery directors–are constantly engaged in altruistic activities that support the community of meditating monks. Thus, in Korea, the two wheels of

wisdom and action run very well together.

My dear Professor, if you look at recorded history, you will see that Buddhists never created conflicts or initiated wars for the sake of their religious beliefs. This fact alone should be proof enough that when people engage in meditation, and through their own efforts reach the home of their mind-nature, the earth becomes a single family. The material and the immaterial are revealed to be nondual and at one with you and me. Since you and I are not two, how then could there be any strife and animosity?

Prof. Knitter: Thank you for this excellent teaching! I have two follow-up questions. One is a personal one for you, Sunim, and the other one is for me. I have a personal question for you: As a Christian, I would like to know a little more about your own path of practice. How did you, in your own life, come to practice the way you do? Please tell me how you come to the experience of enlightenment, so that perhaps I can learn from you, from your own path, and from your own personal experience.

Seon Master Jinje: I joined the Buddhist monastic order when I was twenty years old. After I wrestled with the deep interior questioning on the hwadu for some three or four years, all of sudden I thought that I had reached the truth. I went to see the great Seon Master Hyanggok, so he could examine whether my insight was complete or partial. In those days, Hyanggok Sunim was a great leader and teacher whose own spiritual insights had been sanctioned and who had thus inherited the main lineage of Korean Seon. Entering his room, I prostrated to him three times, and said, "I've come to have my view examined."

Without even a perfunctory greeting, Hyanggok Sunim shouted, "If you speak, I will hit you thirty times with my Seon staff; if you stay silent, I will hit you thirty times with my staff! What do you do?"

I was at a total loss for words! He thundered back, "So you can't even answer this one simple question! How dare you come here, thinking you know something!"

He then he questioned me about a famous story, well known in Seon circles: the story of Nanchuan's cat.

A long time ago in China, some seven hundred illustrious monks practiced Seon meditation in the monastery of Seon Master Nanchuan. The monastery had a cat that was cared for by the monks of both residential wings of the monastery. The monks of the eastern Seon hall claimed the cat as their favorite pet, while the monks of the western Seon Hall claimed the cat as theirs. There were sometime disputes over the proper care and feeding of the monastery cat. So, one day, a huge dispute broke out in the monastery.

Learning of this dispute, Seon Master Nanchuan ordered his attendant to strike the monastery bell, calling all of the monastery residents together. All seven hundred monks dropped what they were doing and gathered in the main Dharma Hall. The Seon Master ascended the Dharma seat and ordered his attendant: "Bring me the cat and a knife."

Lifting the cat with one hand, and holding the knife with the other, Nanchuan exclaimed to the assembly: "All you Seon practitioners have been arguing over a cat. So, in order to resolve this, today I say to you monks of the eastern and western halls: you both claim this cat as your own. Give me one word to save this cat. If you cannot, I will cut the cat in half!"

Seeing this, a great hue and cry went up from the assembly. Some monks shouted, "It's our cat!" Other monks shouted, "It's our cat!" All of them remained stuck in their petty dispute. Since none of them could give a satisfactory answer, Seon Master Nanchuan sliced the cat in two, and returned to his room.

Some hours later, Nanchuan's most accomplished student, Zhaozhou Sunim, returned to the monastery after finishing some business in the market. Seon Master Nanchuan related to him the happenings of the day. "Today I taught the assembly of monks about this cat," Master Nanchuan said. "If you had been there at that time, what would you have done to save that cat?"

Hearing this, Zhaozhou Sunim immediately placed his pair of grass sandals on top of his head, and left the room. Nanchuan sighed and said, "Ah, Zhaozhou Sunim, if only you had been in the assembly we could have saved that cat."

This seemingly inscrutable action on Zhaozhou's part suggests that simply placing a pair of grass sandals on one's head might be an appropriate solution for this difficult question of life and death. So, Seon Master Hyanggok asked me, "Tell me why Zhaozhou Sunim placed a pair of grass sandals on his head and went away?"

I was at a total loss for words. Seon Master Hyanggok threw me out of his room, saying: "You stupid monk! How come you trumpet forth about realizing something when you can't even understand this question?"

From that day on, I practiced Seon meditation for two years at various Seon halls. I strove diligently to prepare my mind to meet a clear-eyed master so that my practice would continue in the right direction. Wandering here and

there like clouds and water, I lived out of my monk's back-pack from retreat season to retreat season.

One day, when I was twenty-six years old, I went to see Seon Master Hyanggok again. I entreated him, "Master, give me a 'hwadu.'"

"How can you get through this Great Barrier, which is so difficult and demanding?" he shot back.

I promised him, "I will devote my whole body and mind to this practice."

Sensing the sincerity of my statement, Hyanggok Sunim

gave me a hwadu. Bowing in eternal gratitude for his intervention and assistance in my study of the self, I said, "I will
not pick up my backpack again to travel until I have broken
through this hwadu."

I grappled with this hwadu for about two years and five
months, struggling with all my heart. Every single day during that period, I woke up at 3 a.m., rolled up my bedding,
and went straight to the Buddha Hall for the morning service. It was always dark outside at that time of night and the
monastery had no exterior lighting. One morning, on the
way to services, I tripped over a paving stone. The moment
I got up, suddenly the hwadu had completely shattered.

In those days, the hwadu that I was using was the case
of Xiangyan climbing a tree. Here is the story behind this
hwadu:

> Someone is dangling by his mouth from a tall tree. His
> hands are tied behind his back and there's nothing beneath
> his feet. Someone appears under the tree and asks him,
> "What is the meaning of Bodhidharma's coming from the
> West?"
>
> If you were to keep your mouth clenched and refuse to
> answer, you will forsake the questioner; but if you open
> your mouth to answer, you will fall to your death. If you

were there, what do you do?"

After tripping over that paving stone, I had broken through the barrier of the hwadu. I composed a Song of Enlightenment and presented it to Seon Master Hyanggok:

> How many people have known this Seon staff?
> None of the sages of past, present, or future recognize it.
> This Seon staff transforms into a golden dragon,
> Its limitless responses, I wield entirely at my own will.

Hyanggok Sunim read the poem, and did not comment of the first two lines. But taking up the next two lines, he threw a question at me like a thunderbolt: "When the dragon meets a Garuda, what will you do?"

In Asian culture, a Garuda is a mythical bird that beats the sea with its wings when it's hungry, splitting sea water 10 miles away; it then dives into the deep sea and snatches the dragons that are under the sea to eat. Hyanggok Sunim was asking me how I would react if I came across this fearsome bird.

So I responded, "I will bend my body at the chest, and move backward three steps."

Suddenly, Seon Master Hyanggok roared back, "Ah, right

you are! Correct!"

Having solved this gongan case, I was free to give Dharma talks and teach. Nothing hindered me in practice or teaching. And yet there was still one gongan I could not break through:

> Seon Master Mazu was close to death. His attendant monk asked after the venerable master's health every morning: "Master, did you sleep well last night?" Mazu Sunim would answer, "Sun-faced Buddha, Moon-faced Buddha."

After relating this story to me one day, Seon Master Hyanggok asked, "Jinje Sunim, what did Master Mazu mean when he said 'Sun-faced Buddha, Moon-faced Buddha'?"

I was at a total loss for words. For some five years, I devoted all my energy to questioning this hwadu.

I had spent nine years practicing Seon meditation at Myogwaneum Monastery. Because that monastery is located in the extreme southern part of the Korean peninsula, it seldom snows. But one morning, during the first month of the year according to the lunar calendar, I saw snow blanketing the hills and the seashore surrounding the monastery. While walking around a corner of a building, I saw a big bucket filled utterly to the brim with water. No snow had accumu-

lated in the bucket because snowflakes melt in water. At that very instant the hwadu shattered.

I broke through this tough hwadu only after a five-year-long effort. I then composed another Enlightenment Gatha and presented it directly to Seon Master Hyanggok:

One strike of this Seon staff topples Vairocana over on his head,

One thunderous shout wipes away the Seon cases of the millions of sages,

In this small thatched hut, I stretch out my legs,

The fresh breeze over the ocean is eternally renewed.

Reading this verse, Seon Master Hyanggok praised me to the hilt, "The deepest meanings of the Sixth Patriarch, Seon Master Mazu, and even Linji's family tradition sing out from these lines!"

In the year of the Fire Goat (1967), Seon Master Hyanggok ascended the high Dharma Seat, and prepared to give a Dharma talk in the Main Buddha Hall of Myogwaneum Monastery. It was the closing ceremony for the 90-day summer intensive retreat. I rose before the assembly, prostrated three times, and said: "Master, I do not want to ask about something the Buddha and Patriarchs know. Would you please tell me instead what the Buddha and Patriarchs don't know?"

Seon Master Hyanggok replied, "Nine times nine is eighty-eight."

"That is what the Buddha and Patriarchs know."

"Six times six is thirty-three."

Upon hearing this, I bowed and departed, without saying whether it was right or wrong. The Seon master continued, "I have completed today's Dharma talk," and promptly descended from the high Dharma seat.

The next day, putting on formal robes, I went to the Seon Master's room and asked again, "I do not ask about the Buddha Eye or the correct Dharma Eye. What is the correct Dharma eye of this patch-robed monk?"

Seon Master Hyanggok replied, "An old Buddhist nun congenitally performs woman's work."

"Today, I saw you in person for the first time," I replied. "For the last nine years, we stayed together and got along in every action. Today, I peeped into your enlightened secret. Ah-ha, so this is what it means!"

Seon Master Hyanggok asked back, "And where did you see me?"

"Gwan! (Blocked!)" I shouted.

With this answer, he sanctioned my endowment of an eye of truth and bestowed on me the Certificate of Authorization he had inherited from the Buddha:

Bestowed to Patriarch Jinje Boepwon
The great living truth [lit. live word] of the buddhas and

patriarchs,

Can be neither transmitted nor received.

Today I entrust this living truth to you,

I leave entirely up to you whether you unveil it or hold it back.

This is the way of transmission in Korean Ganhwa Seon; this is how the essence of Korean Seon is expressed and confirmed. It is a tradition descended from the Buddha until now. This kind of enlightenment tradition is vividly alive only in Korea, not in contemporary China or even Japan.

Prof. Knitter: Well, that kind of prepares me for my second question, which concerns the Dharma name you gave me this morning. My Dharma name is "True Self" (Jin-a), which also serves as my hwadu. I must say that I was very moved when you gave me this name. The notion of true self is also found in the Christian scriptures, in the Bible. We are asked to realize and discover our true selves. But I must say that it is also one of the things that I feel, as a Christian, we can learn from your tradition.

Is hwadu the same as koan practice? You told me that I should keep this question, "What was I before my parents conceived me?" You told me I should keep a ball of doubt and keep asking the question: "Who am I?," "What is my true self?"

So are you telling me just to keep practicing, to keep this question in mind when I am walking, when I am sleeping, and when I am talking–not to lose contact with it during any activity. But should I just wait for enlightenment, then? My question is this (and this may be a typically Christian question): Can I be sure that there will finally be that moment when enlightenment occurs? Can I trust that this will happen before I die?

Seon Master Jinje: The practice of seeing into your True Nature and getting enlightened is possible anytime and anywhere. You should simply raise the question, "What is my True Self before my parents gave birth to me?" Just continue this questioning, day and night, with total devotion and purposefulness, like the mind of a parent yearning to see again their long-lost only son. Then, if you practice in this way, you won't be bothered by what you see and what you hear and you won't have any sense of time passing or of where you are. Anyone, regardless of gender or age, can reach this level. The key to awakening is how long and steady the single-mindedness of the hwadu questioning continues. If the earnest questioning continues on without interruption, you might think that just a moment has passed, but in fact days or months may have already elapsed. When you arrive at this state, you may unexpectedly see or hear something that causes the hwadu to shatter. In that instant, you will have reached the status of a Buddha right where you are standing, without moving a single step. This process can be completed only under the guidance of a clear-eyed enlightened master. You cannot succeed on your own.

Prof. Knitter: So, the Buddha emphasizes the need to realize your true self and then to act. And Jesus is talking about the need to involve yourself for the sake of justice, for the sake of stopping the sufferings of others caused by oppressive political structures. Both approaches are necessary, and I think they both can speak to each other.

Seon Master Jinje: Religions should all aim to guide people to a land of peace and bliss, shouldn't they? Each religion has its own virtue. So, in the future, all religious leaders should strive to find common ground in order to save the world. Thank you very much for your openness and your sincerity, Professor Knitter.

At this point, Seon Master Jinje presented a gift to Prof. Knitter, a calligraphic scroll that he had written.

Seon Master Jinje: (*reading the calligraphy aloud*): "Be a leader wherever you are, and save all sentient beings, far and wide." Presented by Jinje, at Haeun Jeongsa (Ocean Cloud Vihara), to Layman Jin-a (True Self), on the first day of The Year of the Iron Rabbit (2011).

Prof. Knitter: Oh! I cannot find words to express my thanks to you.

Seon Master Jinje: Please take good care of yourself. I wish you a long life! Please strive to guide all people to the land of peace and happiness.

Prof. Knitter: I'll do my best.

There finally was a concluding question from a reporter who was covering the event for the Yeongnam Daily News:

Kim Eungyeong: Modern society is moving inexorably into an age of materialism. I want to ask Venerable Jinje what the true role of religion should be at this time?

Seon Master Jinje: Nowadays, human beings enjoy limitless material affluence. However, humans' desires are also endless. In order to pacify these endless desires, everyone needs to practice Seon meditation in their daily life so as to light up their inner wisdom and bring peace to the world.

You are alive today, but you may die tomorrow. When you lose yourself in endless materialistic pursuits, you will have a miserable life in the next rebirth. Hence, if you cultivate your pure and light mind through meditation practice, you will be reborn in a favorable environment and lead a life of good fortune and bliss.

The ancients used to say, "To live poor is due to a poverty of wisdom. When a horse gets thin, its hair grows long." If you want bright wisdom, social success and fortune, you must devote yourself to the hwadu, "What is my True Self before my parents gave birth to me?" Question yourself in this manner, day and night throughout your everyday routine. If you do so, all the karma of past, present, and future will be purified naturally, and wisdom as bright as the sun and the moon will appear in your mind. This will enable you to lead one wonderful life after another in successive rebirths.

So, when you practice Seon meditation steadily in your everyday life, you will be free from all inner conflicts and will live a carefree life; your family and the whole world will live in peace.

My fellow human beings! I earnestly encourage you to carry out this meditation wonderfully and beautifully. This is my last word, given as a gift to you.

Donghwa Monastery, 31 December 2010

Seon Master Jinje's Transmission Lineage

Seon Master Jinje and the Patriarchs

Seon Master Jinje's Transmission Lineage

The 1st Patriarch Ven. Mahakasyapa (摩訶迦葉)

The 2nd Patriarch Ven. Ananda (阿難尊者)

The 3rd Patriarch Ven. Sanavasin (商那和修)

The 4th Patriarch Ven. Upagupta (優波鞠多)

The 5th Patriarch Ven. Dhritaka (提多迦)

The 6th Patriarch Ven. Micchaka (彌遮迦)

The 7th Patriarch Ven. Vasumitra (婆須密多)

The 8th Patriarch Ven. Buddhanandi (佛陀難提)

The 9th Patriarch Ven. Buddhamitra (伏馱密多)

The 10th Patriarch Ven. Parsva (脇尊者)

The 11th Patriarch Ven. Punyayasas (富那夜奢)

The 12th Patriarch Ven. Asvagosha (馬鳴大師)

The 13th Patriarch Ven. Kapimala (迦毘摩羅)

The 14th Patriarch Ven. Nagarjuna (龍樹大師)

The 15th Patriarch Ven. Kanadeva (迦那提婆)

The 16th Patriarch Ven. Rahulata (羅睺羅多)

The 17th Patriarch Ven. Sanghanandi (僧伽難提)

The 18ᵗʰ Patriarch Ven. Gayasata (伽倻舍多)

The 19ᵗʰ Patriarch Ven. Kumarata (鳩摩羅多)

The 20ᵗʰ Patriarch Ven. Sayata (闍夜多)

The 21ˢᵗ Patriarch Ven. Vasubandhu (婆修盤頭)

The 22ⁿᵈ Patriarch Ven. Manorahita (摩拏羅)

The 23ʳᵈ Patriarch Ven. Haklenayasa (鶴勒那)

The 24ᵗʰ Patriarch Ven. Simhabodhi (師者尊者)

The 25ᵗʰ Patriarch Ven. Vasi Asita (婆舍斯多)

The 26ᵗʰ Patriarch Ven. Puyamitra (不如密多)

The 27ᵗʰ Patriarch Ven. Prajnatara (般若多羅)

Chinese Patriarchs

The 28th Patriarch Ven. Bodhidharma (菩提達磨) (Chinese 1st Patriarch)

The 29th Patriarch Ven. Huike (慧可, Chinese 2nd Patriarch)

The 30th Patriarch Ven. Sengcan (僧璨, Chinese 3rd Patriarch)

The 31st Patriarch Ven. Daoxin (道信, Chinese 4th Patriarch)

The 32nd Patriarch Ven. Hongren (弘忍, Chinese 5th Patriarch)

The 33rd Patriarch Ven. Huineng (慧能, Chinese 6th Patriarch)

The 34th Patriarch Ven. Nanyue Huairang (南嶽懷讓)

The 35th Patriarch Ven. Mazu Daoyi (馬祖道一)

The 36th Patriarch Ven. Baizhang Huaihai (百丈懷海)

The 37th Patriarch Ven. Huangpi Xiyun (黃檗希運)

The 38th Patriarch Ven. Linji Yixuan (臨濟義玄)

The 39th Patriarch Ven. Xinghua Cunjiang (興化存獎)

The 40th Patriarch Ven. Nanyuan Daoyong (南院道顒)

The 41st Patriarch Ven. Fengxue Yanzhao (風穴延沼)

The 42nd Patriarch Ven. Shoushan Xingnian (首山省念)

The 43rd Patriarch Ven. Fenyang Shanzhao (紛陽善昭)

The 44th Patriarch Ven. Ciming Chuyuan (慈明楚圓)

The 45th Patriarch Ven. Yangqi Fanghui (楊岐方會)

The 46th Patriarch Ven. Baiyun Shouduan (白雲守端)

The 47th Patriarch Ven. Wuzu Fayan (五祖法演)

The 48th Patriarch Ven. Yuanwu Keqin (圓悟克勤)

The 49th Patriarch Ven. Huqiu Shaolong (虎丘紹隆)

The 50th Patriarch Ven. Yingyan Tanhua (應庵曇華)

The 51st Patriarch Ven. Miyan Xianjie (密庵咸傑)

The 52nd Patriarch Ven. Poyan Zuxian (破庵祖先)

The 53rd Patriarch Ven. Wuzhun Yuanzhao (無準圓照)

The 54th Patriarch Ven. Xueyan Huillang (雪巖惠朗)

The 55th Patriarch Ven. Jiyan Zongxin (及庵宗信)

The 56th Patriarch Ven. Shiwu Qinggong (石屋清珙)

Korean Patriarchs

The 57th Patriarch Ven. Taego Bou (太古普愚)

The 58th Patriarch Ven. Hwanam Honsu (幻庵混修)

The 59th Patriarch Ven. Gugok Gakun (龜谷覺雲)

The 60th Patriarch Ven. Byeokgye Jeongsim (碧溪淨心)

The 61st Patriarch Ven. Byeoksong Jieom (碧松智嚴)

The 62nd Patriarch Ven. Buyong Yeonggwan (芙蓉靈觀)

The 63rd Patriarch Ven. Cheongheo Hyujeong (淸虛休靜)

The 64th Patriarch Ven. Pyeonyang Eon-gi (鞭羊彦機)

The 65th Patriarch Ven. Pungdam Euisim (楓潭義諶)

The 66th Patriarch Ven. Woldam Seolje (月潭雪霽)

The 67th Patriarch Ven. Hwanseong Jian (喚惺志安)

The 68th Patriarch Ven. Hoam Chejeong (虎巖體淨)

The 69th Patriarch Ven. Cheongbong Geoan (青峰巨岸)

The 70th Patriarch Ven. Yulbong Cheonggo (栗峰青杲)

The 71st Patriarch Ven. Geumheo Beopcheom (錦虛法沾)

The 72nd Patriarch Ven. Yongam Hyeeon (龍岩慧彦)

The 73rd Patriarch Ven. Yeongwol Bongyul (永月奉律)

The 74th Patriarch Ven. Manhwa Boseon (萬化普善)

The 75th Patriarch Ven. Gyeongheo Seongu (鏡虛惺牛)

The 76th Patriarch Ven. Hyewol Hyemyeong (慧月慧明)

The 77th Patriarch Ven. Unbong Seongsu (雲峰性粹)

The 78th Patriarch Ven. Hyanggok Hyerim (香谷蕙林)

The 79th Patriarch Ven. Jinje Beopwon (眞際法遠)

Profile of Seon Master Jinje

1934   Born in Namhae, South Gyeongsang Province, Repub-
        lic of Korea

1954   Enters Haein Monastery, receives novice ordination
        from Seon Master Seoku

1957   Receives full bhiksu ordination at Tongdo Monastery

1959   Begins practice under guidance of Seon Master Hyang-
        gok

1967   Receives Dharma transmission from Master Hyanggok,
        continuing the lineage of masters Gyeongheo, Hye-
        wol, Unbong, and Hyanggok. Recognized in Korea as
        the 79th Patriarch in the dharma lineage deriving from
        Sakyamuni Buddha.

1971   Founded the monastery of Haeun Jeongsa

1979   Josil (Guiding Seon Master) of Geumo Seon Hall at
        Haeun Jeongsa

1991   Chairman of the Board, Institute of Seon Studies. Ap-
        pointed Josil (Guiding Seon Master) of Central Seon
        Center

1994   Josil (Guiding Seon Master) of Donghwa Monastery

1996   Appointed Josil (Guiding Seon Master) of the "Funda-
        mental Seon Practice," responsible for overseeing the
        Seon training of meditation monks in the Jogye Order

of Korean Buddhism.

1998   Invited to be a presiding Seon Master for the First Open Seon Conference, held at Baekyang Monastery

2000   Invited to be a presiding Seon Master for the Second Open Seon Conference, held at Baekyang Monastery

2000   Invited to be Josil (Guiding Seon Master) of the Taego Seon Hall at Bongam Monastery

2002   Presiding Seon Master of the International Open Seon Conference, held at Haeun Jeongsa

2003   Becomes a member of the Council of Elders, Jogye Order of Korean Buddhism

2004   Awarded the title of Daejongsa, "most eminent monk," by the Jogye Order of Korean Buddhism

2009   Presiding Seon Master of the "Hundred-Seat Dharma Assembly" held in the BEXCO Center, Busan, South Korea